THE ORIGINS OF GREEK THOUGHT

Jean-Pierre Vernant

Translated from the French

CORNELL UNIVERSITY PRESS

Ithaca, New York

Published in France as *Les origines de la pensée grecque* by Presses Universitaires de France. © 1962, Presses Universitaires de France.

Translation copyright © 1982 by Cornell University Press

First published 1982 by Cornell University Press
First printing, Cornell Paperbacks, 1984

Printed in the United States of America

Library of Congress Cataloging-in-Publication Data

Vernant, Jean Pierre.
The origins of Greek thought.

Translation of: Les origines de la pensée grecque
Bibliography: p.
Includes index.
1. Civilization, Greek.   2. Philosophy, Ancient.   I. Title
DF78.V4813   938   81-15247
ISBN-13: 978-0-8014-9293-8 (pbk.: alk. paper) AACR2
ISBN-10: 0-8014-9293-9 (pbk.: alk. paper)

Cornell University Press strives to use environmentally responsible suppliers and materials to the fullest extent possible in the publishing of its books. Such materials include vegetable-based, low-VOC inks and acid-free papers that are recycled, totally chlorine-free, or partly composed of nonwood fibers. For further information, visit our website at www.cornellpress.cornell.edu.

Paperback printing   10

THE ORIGINS OF
GREEK THOUGHT

FOR LOUIS GERNET

Contents

Introduction

With the deciphering of the Mycenaean Linear B script, the date of the first Greek texts available to us receded by half a millennium. This deepening of chronological perspective alters the entire framework in which the problem of the origins of Hellenic thought is set. The earliest Greek world, as the Mycenaean tablets conjure it up for us, is allied in many ways with the contemporaneous Near Eastern kingdoms. The same type of social organization, a similar way of life, and a similar human being are revealed in the Linear B writings of Knossos, Pylos, and Mycenae and in the cuneiform archives found at Ugarit, Alalakh, Mari, and the Hittite Hattusas. But as one begins to read Homer, the picture changes: the *Iliad* reveals another society, a different human world, as though by the Homeric age the Greeks could no longer fully comprehend the features of the Mycenaean civilization to which they were connected and which, through the epic poets, they believed they were evoking out of the past.

This break in Greek history is one we should try to

understand and locate with precision. The religion and mythology of classical Greece, as M. P. Nilsson in particular has shown, are unmistakably rooted in the Mycenaean past.[1] But in other areas the rupture appears complete. When Mycenaean power crumbled under the pressure of the Dorian tribes that invaded mainland Greece in the twelfth century before our era, it was not a dynasty alone that perished in the conflagration that consumed first Pylos and then Mycenae. A type of kingship was destroyed forever, a whole form of social life centered on the palace. A person, the divine king, vanished from the Greek horizon. The collapse of the Mycenaean system had consequences that extended far beyond the realm of political and social history. In changing their spiritual universe, transforming certain of their psychological attitudes, it had repercussions on the Greeks themselves. The king's disappearance prepared the way, through the long and murky period of isolation and reconstruction we call the Dark Age of Greece, for two interdependent innovations: the institution of the city-state and the birth of rational thought. In Europe and Ionia toward the end of the Geometric period (900–750 B.C.), the Greeks resumed relations with the Orient, which had been suspended for several centuries. When

[1]Martin P. Nilsson, *The Minoan-Mycenaean Religion and Its Survival in Greek Religion,* 2d ed. (Lund, 1950). See also Charles Picard, *Les religions préhelléniques* (Paris, 1948) and "La formation du polythéisme hellénique et les récents problèmes relatifs au linéaire B," in *Eléments orientaux dans la religion grecque ancienne* (Paris, 1960), pp. 163–177; G. Pugliese Carratelli, "Riflessi di culti micenei nelle tabelle di Cnosso a Pilo," in *Studi in onore de U. E. Paoli* (Florence, 1955), pp. 1–16; L. A. Stella, "La religione greca nei testi micenei," in *Numen,* 5 (1958), 18–57.

they rediscovered certain aspects of their own Bronze Age past in the civilizations that flourished there, they did not embark on immigration and assimilation, as the Mycenaeans had done. In the midst of a full Orientalizing revival, Hellenism affirmed itself as such, in counterpoise to Asia, as though renewed contact with the East had brought it greater self-awareness. The Greeks found themselves with a certain form of social life and a kind of thought that in their own eyes constituted their originality and their superiority to the barbarian world: in place of the king who wielded his omnipotence without control or limit in the privacy of his palace, Greek political life aimed to become the subject of public debate, in the broad daylight of the agora, between citizens who were defined as equals and for whom the state was the common undertaking. In place of the old cosmogonies associated with royal rituals and myths of sovereignty, a new thought sought to base the order of the world on relations of symmetry, equilibrium, and equality among the various elements that made up the cosmos.

If we wish to document the birth of this Greek rationality, to follow the path by which it managed to divest itself of a religious mentality, to indicate what it owed to myth and how far it went beyond it, we must compare and contrast with its Mycenaean background that turning point, from the eighth to the seventh century, where Greece made a new start and began to explore paths that were peculiarly its own: a period of decisive mutation that laid the foundations for the government of the *polis* at the very moment when the Orientalizing style was triumphant, and which ensured the advent of philosophy by secularizing political thought.

THE ORIGINS OF
GREEK THOUGHT

CHAPTER ONE

The Historical Background

At the beginning of the second millennium, the shores of the Mediterranean did not yet mark a division between East and West. With no discontinuity of people or culture, the Aegean world and the Hellenic peninsula were linked on the one hand to the Anatolian plateau, by way of the Cyclades and the Sporades, and on the other to Mesopotamia and Iran by way of Rhodes, Cilicia, Cyprus, and the northern coast of Syria. When Crete emerged from the Cycladic era, during which relations with Anatolia had predominated and the first palace-centered civilizations had been founded at Phaistos, Mallia, and Knossos (2000–1700 B.C.), it was still oriented toward the great kingdoms of the Near East. The resemblances between the Cretan palaces and those recently excavated at Alalakh, at the bend of the Orontes, and at Mari, on the caravan route from Mesopotamia to the sea, are so striking as to suggest the work of architects and painters who belonged to the same school.[1] By way of the Syrian coast

[1] See Leonard Woolley, *A Forgotten Kingdom* (London, 1953), and André Parrot, *Mission archéologique de Mari* (Paris, 1958), II.

the Cretans also came into contact with the Egypt of the New Empire, whose influence, though less decisive than was supposed in Evans' time, is nevertheless well attested.

Between 2000 and 1900 B.C. a new population invaded mainland Greece. Its buildings and burial sites, its war axes, its bronze weapons, its implements and pottery—the typical gray Minyan ware—all show a break with the people and the civilization of the previous era, the Early Helladic age. The invaders, the Minyans, formed the vanguard of the tribes that in successive waves settled in Hellas, installed themselves on the islands, colonized the coast of Asia Minor, and pushed on toward the western Mediterranean and the Black Sea, thus forming the Greek world as it is known to history. Whether they came down from the Balkans or over from the plains of southern Russia, these ancestors of the Greeks were an Indo-European people, already differentiated by language, and speaking a dialect of archaic Greek. Their appearance on the shores of the Mediterranean is no isolated phenomenon. A parallel thrust was apparent around the same time from the other side of the Mediterranean, when the Indo-European Hittites arrived in Asia Minor and spread across the Anatolian plateau. In the Troad, along the coast, the cultural and ethnic continuity that had been maintained for nearly a millennium, from Troy I (which had its beginnings between 3000 and 2600 B.C.) to Troy V, was suddenly disrupted. The people who built Troy VI (1900 B.C.), a princely city richer and more powerful than any before it, were closely related to the Minyans of Greece. They made the same gray ware, turned on a potter's wheel and baked in closed ovens, that was to be found in mainland Greece, the Ionian islands, Thessaly, and Chalcidice.

Another cultural element underscores the similarity of the peoples on the opposite shores of the Mediterranean: it is with the people of Troy VI that the horse makes its appearance in the Troad. The epithet "rich in horses," in the formulaic style borrowed by Homer from an ancient oral tradition, still calls up the splendor of the Dardanians. The fame of Troy's horses, as of its fabrics, was surely not unrelated to the interest the Achaeans took in that region even before the warring expedition that destroyed Priam's city (Troy VIIa) and thus launched the epic legend of the Trojan War. Like the Minyans of the Troad, those of Greece were acquainted with the use of horses and must have raised them on the steppes where they had sojourned before their arrival in Greece. The evolution of the worship of Poseidon shows that before his advent as god of the sea, there had been an equine Poseidon—Hippos or Hippios—in whom, among the first Hellenes as among other peoples, the idea of the horse was part of an entire mythological complex: the horse is associated with moisture, with subterranean waters, the underworld, fertility; with wind, storm, cloud, tempest . . . .[2] The horse's place, importance, and prestige in any society arise largely from its military function. The earliest Greek documents we have that shed any light on this matter date from the sixteenth century: funerary stelae unearthed in the circle of shaft graves at Mycenae (1580–1500) depict battle or hunting scenes in

[2]See F. Schachermeyr, *Poseidon und die Entstehung des Griechischen Götterglaubens* (Bern, 1948).

which a warrior stands on a chariot drawn by galloping horses. At that period the Minyans, having intermingled with a local population of Asian origin, had long been established in mainland Greece, where urban life sprang up at the bases of the fortress-residences of chieftains. They had already made contact with Minoan Crete, in full flower after the revival that followed the reconstruction of the palaces, which had been destroyed for the first time around 1700. Crete had revealed to them a way of life and thought that was entirely new. A gradual Cretanizing of the Mycenaean world was already under way, and after 1450 led to a common palace-centered civilization on the island and in mainland Greece. But the war chariot, a light cart drawn by two horses, cannot have been of Cretan origin. The horse did not appear on the island before Late Minoan I (1580–1450). If any borrowing was done here, the Minoans were the debtors. On the other hand, the use of chariots does reveal a similarity between the Mycenaean or Achaean world, just then arising, and the kingdom of the Hittites, who around the sixteenth century adopted it as a battle tactic from the Hurrians of Mitanni, their neighbors to the east—a non-Indo-European population that nonetheless acknowledged the rule of an Indo-Iranian dynasty. Even to a people accustomed to the raising of horses, chariotry must have posed new problems of selection and training. We find a hint of such concerns in a treatise on horses by a certain Kikkuli, of the land of the Mitanni, which was translated into Hittite. Concerns of this sort played a part in the relations established at the beginning of the fourteenth century between the Hittites and the people they called the Achaiwoi (the Achaeans or Mycenaeans).

Among other references to Ahhiyawa (Achaea), the Hittite royal archives of Hattusas mention the brief stay of certain Achaean princes, among them Tawagalawas (Eteokles?), who had come to the court to improve themselves in the use of chariots. Ought we to place alongside the name of the Hittite king Mursilis that of Myrtilus, Oenomaus' charioteer, who is known to us for his role in the legend of Pelops, ancestor of the Atreid dynasty, rulers of Mycenae?

Oenomaus ruled at Pisa in Elis. He had a daughter, Hippodameia. Any man who wished to marry her would have to win her in a chariot race against her father. Defeat meant death. Many suitors had come forward, and all had been outrun by the king, whose horses were invincible. The suitors' heads now adorned the walls of the palace. With Hippodameia's aid, Pelops bribed Myrtilus, the king's charioteer, so that in the middle of the race Oenomaus' chariot crashed, its axle sabotaged. Thus Pelops won the chariot race—a victory that won him both the daughter, Tamer-of-Horses, and the kingship. As for Myrtilus, the overclever and enterprising charioteer, Pelops disposed of him in due course, and the gods then transformed him into the constellation Auriga.

This tale of qualifying for kingship puts the chariot race under the patronage of Poseidon, the old horse god, who by that period of Mycenaean civilization was no longer a pastoral figure, but a master of the chariot, a warrior-aristocrat. Indeed, the finish line at Corinth was marked by an altar to Poseidon the horse god (Poseidon Hippios and Damaios), which consecrated the victor on his arrival. And the myth closely associates Pelops with Poseidon in yet another way. As a youth he underwent

19

an initiation rite in which he was killed and served up in a dish to his father. He then was reborn and promptly abducted by Poseidon. The god made Pelops his page, in keeping with the archaic practice that was still followed by the martial fraternities of Crete, and of which we are informed by Strabo, who drew upon Ephorus.[3] The abduction was part of a strict protocol: presents were offered by the abductor, and the youth then became his companion for a two-month period of isolation. Upon his release the boy received a prescribed set of gifts: his battle dress, an ox, and a cup. Poseidon also made Pelops a gift that was symbolic of the powers the youth had gained by his intimacy with the god: a chariot.

The handling of the chariot required a strenuous apprenticeship, which must have reinforced the military specialization that was typical of the social organization and outlook of the Indo-Europeans. Then, too, the possession of a large reserve of chariots to mass on the battlefield presupposes a centralized state of such size and power that the charioteers, whatever their prerogatives, were subject to a single authority.

Such military strength must in fact have been possessed by the kingdom of Mycenae, which by 1450 (as we have known since the decipherment of Linear B) was able to dominate Crete, take control of the palace at Knossos, and hold it until its final destruction in the conflagration of 1400—a conflagration possibly ignited by a local revolt. The Mycenaean expansion, which continued in the western Mediterranean between the fourteenth and

[3]Strabo, X, 483c; see Louis Gernet, "Droit et prédroit en Grèce ancienne," L'Année sociologique, 1951, pp. 389ff.

twelfth centuries, brought in the Achaeans, who took over from the Cretans and replaced them nearly everywhere, though with certain time lags here and there. As early as the dawn of the fourteenth century they had colonized Rhodes. It is perhaps on that island, safe from attack from the continent, that we should place the kingdom of Ahhiyawa, whose ruler was treated by the Hittite king with the respect due an equal. From Rhodes the Achaean king could oversee the several points on the Anatolian coast where his men had gained footholds and established settlements. The Achaean presence is attested at Miletus (the Hittite Milawunda or Milawata), at Colophon, at Claros, farther north at Lesbos, notably in the Troad, with which relations were close, and finally on the more southerly coasts of Cilicia and Pamphilia. By the beginning of the fourteenth century the Mycenaeans had also installed themselves in force on Cyprus, and at Enkomi they built a fortress similar to those in the Argolid. From there they reached the Syrian coast, which offered access to Mesopotamia and Egypt. In the fifteenth century a Cretan colony at Ugarit, where copper was traded with Cyprus, left its mark on the city's culture and even on its architecture. In the following century that colony gave way to a Mycenaean settlement well enough supplied to take possession of its own quarter of the city. In the same period, Alalakh, on the Orontes, gateway to the Euphrates and Mesopotamia, became an important Achaean center. Farther south, Achaeans made their way as far as Phoenicia, Byblos, and Palestine. In the whole region a common Cypro-Mycenaean civilization was developing—one in which Mycenaean-Minoan and

21

Asian elements were closely intermingled, and which used a script that was derived, like the Mycenaean syllabary, from the Cretan Linear A. Egypt, which had carried on continuous trade with the Cretans, most notably during the fifteenth century, welcomed the Mycenaeans and gave them free access between 1400 and 1340. There, once again, the Keftiou, or Cretans, were eliminated little by little in favor of their competitors, until Crete ceased to play the role of intermediary between Egypt and the Greek mainland, as it had done earlier. Perhaps a Mycenaean colony was present at El-Amarna when Amenhotep IV, under the name of Akhnaton, took up residence there between 1380 and 1350 after he abandoned the ancient capital of Thebes.

Thus in all the regions where their spirit of adventure led them, the Mycenaeans appear to have been closely associated with the major civilizations of the eastern Mediterranean and to have been integrated into this Near Eastern world, which for all its diversity constituted a whole, thanks to its breadth of contact, exchange, and communications.

CHAPTER TWO

Mycenaean Royalty

Decipherment of the Linear B tablets has answered certain questions asked by archaeologists, but it has also posed new ones. In addition to the usual problems of interpretation, Linear B is difficult to read because, having been derived from a syllabic writing not designed for use in setting down Greek, it renders very imperfectly the sounds of the Mycenaeans' own spoken dialect. Then, too, the number of documents we have is still limited: we have not laid our hands on actual archives, but rather on some annual inventories inscribed on clay tablets, which would doubtless have been erased to be used again if they had not been baked, and thus preserved, in the fire that destroyed the palaces. A single example will suffice to show the gaps in our information and the precautions that are called for. The word *te-re-ta*, which recurs often in the texts, has been interpreted at least four ways: priest; man in feudal service, or baron; man of the *damos* [community] subject to taxation; and servant. We are therefore unable to draw a picture of Mycenaean social organization. Nevertheless, the differing views of that organization, even the most contradictory, agree on some points that can be considered reasonably well established, given the current state of our sources.

Social life appears to have been centered on the palace, whose function was at once religious, political, military, administrative, and economic. In this palace-centered economic system, as it has been called, the king brought together and fused in his own person all aspects of power and sovereignty. Through the agency of the scribes, who formed a professional class established by tradition, and a complex hierarchy of palace dignitaries and royal inspectors, the king controlled and closely regulated all sectors of economic life and all spheres of social activity.

The scribes preserved in their archives an account of everything that had to do with livestock and agriculture; the tenure of land, which was evaluated in measures of grain (for both tax rates and seed rations); the specialized trades, with allocations of raw materials to be furnished and orders for finished products; workers available or employed; slaves—men, women, and children—both those who were privately owned and those who belonged to the king; taxes of every sort levied by the palace against persons and communities, goods already delivered and those still outstanding; levies of men to be supplied by certain villages to row the royal vessels; the composition, command, and movement of military units; sacrifices to the gods, the standard rates specified for offerings, and so on.

In this kind of economy there seems to be no room for private commerce. Terms do exist for "to acquire" and "to dispose of," but we find no evidence of a form of payment in gold or silver, or of a recognized equivalence between merchandise and precious metals. The royal administration seems to have regulated distribution and exchange, as it did the production of goods. Products, labor, and services—all equally codified and accounted for—were circulated and interchanged, linking together the various elements of the country, through the central agency of the palace, which controlled the double circuit of provisioning and reimbursement.

This has been called a bureaucratic royalty. Though the connotations of the term are much too modern, it emphasizes one aspect of a system that is led by its own logic to a control more and more rigorous, more and more oppressive, as it takes note of details that to us seem insignificant. It invites comparison with the great riverine states of the Near East, whose organization appears to have been at least in part a response to the need to coordinate on a vast scale the labor of draining, irrigating, and maintaining the canals that were indispensable to agriculture. Were the Mycenaean kingdoms obliged to deal with similar problems? The draining of Lake Copais was in fact undertaken during the Mycenaean period. But what was the situation on the plains of the Argolid, Messenia, and Attica? One would not have thought that in Greece the technical requirements of developing the land in accordance with an overall plan could have given rise to or favored such administrative centralization. The rural economy of ancient Greece appears to have been fragmented at the village level; coordination of labor hardly extended beyond a group of neighbors.

It is not only in the agricultural realm that the Mycenaean world differs from the riverine civilizations of

25

the Near East. While recognizing the pivotal role of the palace in social life, L. R. Palmer has pointed to the features that link Mycenaean society with the Indo-European world. Especially striking is the analogy with the Hittites, who in the process of becoming Orientalized still preserved certain distinctive practices connected with their military organization. Assembled around the king in the large Hittite household were the people closest to him—palace dignitaries whose titles indicate high administrative functions, but who also exercised military authority. Together with the units under their command, they formed the *pankus*, the assembly that represented the Hittite community—that is, brought together the body of warriors, as distinct from the rest of the population, according to the Indo-European pattern, in which the warrior is set apart from the villager, the herdsman, and the farmer. These warrior-aristocrats constituted a separate class, and at least the chief of its members were supported on their holdings by peasants bound to the land. It was among these men that the charioteers, the principal force of the Hittite army, were recruited. The institution of the *pankus* may originally have exercised extensive powers: the monarchy may originally have been elective. Later, to avoid crises of succession, ratification of the new king may have been withdrawn from the assembly of warriors, and the *pankus*—which is mentioned for the last time in a proclamation of King Telepinus at the end of the sixteenth century—may at last have become obsolete. Hittite royalty would thus have approximated the model of the absolute monarchies of the East, which relied less on a class of nobles whose political prerogatives were based on military service than on a hierarchy of administrators directly dependent on the king.[1]

The Hittite example has been invoked by scholars who contrast the "bureaucratic" interpretation of Mycenaean royalty with a pattern that makes room for features they describe as "feudal." In reality, both terms seem equally inadequate and in their very contrast anachronistic. At every level of the palace administration, it was in fact a personal bond of allegiance that connected the various palace dignitaries with the king: they were not functionaries in the service of the state, but servants of the king, charged with manifesting, wherever he chose to place them, that absolute power of command which was embodied in the monarch. Thus alongside an often very elaborate division of tasks, a functional specialization with a long series of supervisors and chief supervisors, we see in the palace-centered economy a lack of precision in administrative assignments: they overlap one another, with each of the king's representatives exercising at his own level a delegated authority that in principle covers all of social life with no limitation.

So the problem is not to contrast the concepts of bureaucratic royalty and feudal monarchy, but rather to note, behind those elements common to all societies with a palace-centered economic system, the features that define the Mycenaean case in particular, and which perhaps explain why in Greece a sovereignty of this type did not outlast the fall of the Achaean dynasties.

From this perspective, comparison with the Hittites can be fruitful. It brings out in full relief the differences

[1]See O. R. Gurney, *The Hittites* (London, 1952).

27

that separate the Mycenaean world from the palace-centered civilization of Crete that was its model. The contrast between the two forms of rule is written in the architecture of their palaces.[2] Those of Crete, a maze of rooms laid out in apparent disorder around a central courtyard, are built on a level with the surrounding countryside, onto which they open, unprotected, with wide roads converging on the palace. The Mycenaean manor, centered on the megaron [a great central hall] and the throneroom, is a walled fortress, a chieftain's den, dominating and keeping watch over the plain at its feet. Constructed to withstand a siege, this citadel sheltered the quarters of the king's intimate associates, the military leaders and palace dignitaries, alongside the princely dwelling and its outbuildings. Its military role appears above all to have been defensive: it protected the royal treasury. Here, along with the reserves normally superintended, stocked, and distributed by the palace in the region's economic plan, were gathered precious goods of a different sort, the products of a luxury trade: jewelry, cups, tripods, bowls, the work of goldsmiths, ornamented weapons, metal molds, rugs, embroidered fabrics. Symbols of power, instruments of personal prestige—in their opulence they were a fitting expression of royalty. They were the substance of a lavish commerce that reached far beyond the kingdom's boundaries. Articles received as gifts and to be given in turn, they sealed matrimonial and political alliances, created obligations of

[2]J. D. S. Pendlebury, *A Handbook to the Palace of Minos: Knossos with Its Dependencies* (London, 1954); George E. Mylonas, *Ancient Mycenae* (London, 1957).

service, rewarded vassals, established bonds of hospitality even in distant lands. They were also objects of competition and conflict: one might receive such things as gifts, or win them in battle; it was to lay hands on such treasures that a military expedition was launched, a town destroyed. More than other forms of wealth, finally, they lent themselves to individual appropriation that could survive even death; placed beside the body, as "appurtenances" of the deceased, they followed him into the tomb.[3]

From the evidence of the tablets, we can be specific about this picture of the Mycenaean court and palace. At the apex of the social structure, the king bore the title of *wa-na-ka* (*wanax*). His authority appears to have been exercised at every level of military life. The palace regulated the orders for weapons, the outfitting of chariots, the levying of troops, and the staffing, composition, and movement of fighting units. But the king's powers were no more limited to warfare than they were to the economic sphere. The *wanax* was responsible for religious life; he closely regulated the calendar, watched over the observance of ritual and the celebration of the festivals in honor of the various gods, designated the animals that were to be sacrificed, the plant offerings that were to be made, the offerings due from each citizen according to rank. We may assume that if the royal power was exercised in this way in every area, it was because the sover-

---

[3]Note the distinction between *ktemata* (goods acquired by the individual that were his to dispose of freely—notably his share of booty) and *patroia* (goods belonging to the family group, and not transferrable).

eign, as such, had a special relationship with the religious realm, which in turn was associated with a priestly class that appears to have been numerous and powerful.[4] In support of this hypothesis, we may observe that in Greece the memory of royalty's religious function was perpetuated even in the city framework, and that the memory of the divine king—magician, master of the weather, and controller of fertility—survived there in mythic form. The Cretan legend of Minos, who every nine years entered the cave of Mount Ida to undergo the ordeal that renewed his royal power through direct contact with Zeus,[5] corresponds to the ordeal that the ephors of Sparta imposed on their two kings every nine years, secretly scanning the night skies to read there whether the sovereigns had committed any error that would disqualify them from exercising the royal function. We may also think of the Hittite king, who would abandon the leadership of his armies in the midst of a campaign if his religious obligations required him to return to the capital on a certain date to perform the rites with which he was charged.

Next to the *wa-na-ka*, the second person of the kingdom was the *la-wa-ge-tas*, the leader of the *laos* (literally, the people with weapons, the assembly of warriors). The companions in arms, the *e-qe-ta* (*hepetai*; cf. the Homeric *hetairoi*), who wore an outer garment of a special design as a uniform, were the palace dignitaries who formed the king's retinue, as in the large Hittite household; at the same time they were heads of an *okha* (a military unit) or

[4]See M. Lejeune, "Prêtres et prêtresses dans les documents mycéniens," in *Hommage à Georges Dumézil, Latomus,* 45, 129–139.
[5]*Odyssey,* XIX, 179.

officers charged with liaison between the court and local commanders. The *te-re-ta (telestai)* perhaps also belonged to the *laos*, if we agree with Palmer that these were men in feudal service, enfeoffed barons. Three of these men, according to a tablet from Pylos, were important enough to have the benefits of a *temenos*, a privilege of the *wa-na-ka* and the *la-wa-ge-tas*.[6] *Temenos*, in the language of the epics—in which it is the only Mycenaean term having to do with land that has survived—designated an estate, arable or planted to vineyards, that was offered to the king, to the gods, or to some important person, together with the peasants attached to it, in return for exceptional services or deeds in war.

The ambiguity of a great many terms is further obscured by the complexity of the system of land tenure.[7] Full possession of an estate, like its usufruct, seems to have entailed a multitude of services and payments. It is often difficult to decide whether a term has purely technical significance (uncultivated land, land under cultivation, grazing land converted to arable, land of greater or lesser area) or is an index of social status. A contrast is clearly marked, however, between two types of tenure,

[6]The interpretation of this tablet is in dispute. Other documents tend rather to link the *te-re-ta* closely to the *damos*, in which event it would have to do with peasants subject to taxes.

[7]The complexity of the system of land tenure is suggested by the vocabulary, which is highly specialized and includes many terms that remain obscure. Scholars have debated the meaning of such words as *ka-ma, ko-to-no-o-ko, wo-wo,* and *o-na-to*. The last term denotes a tenancy, although we cannot say exactly what forms it took. On the other hand, we may assume that where the communal land of the *damos* is concerned, the tablets mention only conveyances of it, either temporary or permanent. Finally, was there a population of serfs attached to the land, apart from the *damos* and the slaves? We cannot say.

31

indicating the two different forms that a *ko-to-na* (a share or portion of land) could take. The *ki-ti-me-na ko-to-na* were private estates that had been appropriated, in contrast to the *ke-ke-me-na ko-to-na*, which were attached to the *damos,* the common lands of the village demes—that is, the collective property of the rural group, cultivated in accordance with the open-field system and perhaps periodically redistributed. On this point L. R. Palmer has offered a useful comparison with the Hittite code, which similarly distinguished two sorts of holdings. That of the man in feudal service, the warrior, was a direct dependency of the palace, and reverted to the palace when his service was no longer due. On the other hand, the "men of tools"—that is, the artisans—had the use of what were known as "village lands," which the rural collective granted them for a time and took back when they left.[8] We may draw on data from India that indicate a similar arrangement: on one hand the *vaisya,* the farmer or villager (*vis,* cf. Latin *vicus,* Greek *oikos,* group of houses), on the other the *ksatrya,* the warrior (from *ksatram,* power, possession), the man with an individual holding. In the same way, the Mycenaean baron is the man of the *ki-ti-me-na ko-to-na,* the appropriated land, as distinguished from the common land of the village. In Mycenaean society, then, the two forms of land tenure reveal a more basic polarity: over against the palace, the court, and all those who depended on it, either directly or

[8]See Palmer's interpretation of the Greek word *demiurgos:* not "one employed in the public sphere," but "one who farms a village plot"; for a contrary view, see Kentaro Murakawa, "Demiurgos," *Historia,* 6 (1957), 385–415.

for the holding of their fiefs, we catch a glimpse of a rural society organized into villages with a life of their own. These village "demes" had at their disposal a part of the lands on which they were established; in accordance with traditions and the local hierarchies, they settled the problems presented at their level by agricultural labor, grazing activity, and relations among neighbors. In this provincial setting, contrary to every expectation, appears the person who bears the title we would normally translate as "king": the *pa-si-re-u*, Homer's *basileus*. He was not actually a king who lived in a palace, but rather the lord of a rural estate and a vassal of the *wanax*. This tie of vassalage, in an economic system in which everything was accounted for, took on the form of an administrative responsibility as well: we find the *basileus* overseeing the distribution of allotments of bronze to the blacksmiths in his territory, who were in the palace's employ. And he himself, of course, with the other rich men of the area, contributed a strictly established share to these supplies of metal.[9] Besides the *basileus*, a Council of Elders, the *ke-ro-si-ja* (*gerousia*), confirms the relative autonomy of the village group. Doubtless the heads of the most powerful families sat on this assembly. Ordinary villagers, men of the *damos* in the proper meaning of the term, who supplied the army with foot soldiers and who (to adopt the Homeric formula) counted no more in the council

[9]The assimilation of the *pa-si-re-u* into the *basileus* has recently been questioned. Palmer believes he was a provincial officer in charge of teams of metalworkers employed by the palace; see L. R. Palmer, "Linear B Texts of Economic Interest," *Serta Philologica Aenipontana*, 7–8 (1961), 1–12.

than in war, were at best spectators, listening in silence to those who were authorized to speak and expressing their feelings only by a murmur of approval or displeasure.

Associated with the *basileus* was another person, the *ko-re-te*, who seems to have been a sort of village leader. We may wonder whether this duality of leadership at the local level does not correspond to the duality we have noted in the palace context: the *basileus'* prerogatives, like those of the *wanax*, may have been principally religious (here we may anticipate the *phylobasileis* of classical Greece); the *ko-re-te*, like the *la-wa-ge-tas*, may have exercised a military function.

The term is related to *koiros*, armed band; it appears to have the meaning of the Homeric *koiranos*, which forms a doublet with *hegemon*, but which in association with *basileus* seems to indicate, if not an opposition, at any rate a difference of plane. In fact, a man by the name of Klumenos, *ko-re-te* of the village of I-te-re-wa and a dependent of the palace of Pylos, appears on another tablet as commander of a military unit; a third tablet gives him the qualifier *mo-ro-pa* (*moiropas*, owner of a *moira*, or portion of land).[10]

However incomplete our information, it seems possible to draw some general conclusions about the characteristic features of Mycenaean royalty.

1. First, their warlike aspect. The *wanax* was supported by a warrior aristocracy, the charioteers, who

---

[10]Martin S. Ruiperez, "KO-RE-TE et PO-RO-KO-RO-TE-RE, Remarques sur l'organisation militaire mycénienne," *Etudes mycéniennes: Actes du Colloque international sur les textes mycéniens*, pp. 105–120. For a contrary view, see J. Taillardat, "Notules mycéniennes: Mycénien Ko-re-te et homérique Καλήτωρ," *Revue des Etudes grecques*, 73 (1960), 1–5.

were subject to his authority but who formed a privileged group within the kingdom's social body and military organization, with its own status and its own way of life.

2. The rural communities were not so absolutely dependent on the palace that they could not exist without it. If royal authority had been abolished, the *damos* would have continued to work the same lands by the same methods. As in the past, but within what would now have been a purely village framework, it would have had to support the kings and men of wealth of the locality by deliveries of goods, presents, and more or less obligatory payments.

3. The palace organization, with its administrative personnel, its bookkeeping and registration techniques, its strict regulation of economic and social life, has the look of something borrowed. The whole system rests on the use of writing and the keeping of records. Cretan scribes who had entered the service of the Mycenaean dynasties had adapted the script in use at the palace of Knossos (Linear A) to the dialect of their new masters (Linear B), and in doing so had given them the means of introducing to mainland Greece the administrative methods of the palace-centered economy. The extraordinary sameness of the language of the tablets over time (more than a century and a half separates the documents from Knossos and those from Pylos)[11] and across space (Knossos, Pylos, Mycenae, but also Tiryns, Thebes, Orchomenos) shows that we are dealing with a tradi-

[11] If one accepts A. J. Evans' dating of the documents of Knossos. On the controversy between L. R. Palmer and S. Hood on this point, see J. Raison, "Une controverse sur la chronologie cnossienne," *Bull. de l'Ass. Guillaume Budé*, 1961, pp. 305–319.

tion kept within a strictly closed group. The specialized circles of Cretan scribes furnished the Mycenaean kings with the staff as well as the techniques to administer their palaces.

The palace-centered system offered the Greek sovereigns a remarkable instrument of power. It allowed the state to establish rigorous supervision over a wide territory. It tapped all the wealth of the country and heaped it in the hands of the monarch; it concentrated the important resources and military forces under a single management. It thus made possible the Greeks' great adventures abroad, where they either established themselves in new territories or went in search of the metal and other products that the Greek mainland lacked. The palace-centered economic system appears to be intimately related both to Mycenaean expansion throughout the Mediterranean and to the development in Greece itself, alongside its agricultural life, of a craft enterprise that had already become highly specialized, and which was organized into guilds according to the eastern model.

All this was destroyed by the Dorian invasion, which broke for centuries the ties between Greece and the East. With Mycenae overthrown, the sea ceased to be an access route and became a barrier. Isolated and turned in on itself, the Greek mainland reverted to a purely agricultural economy. The Homeric world was no longer familiar with a division of labor comparable to that of the Mycenaean world, or with the use of slave labor on so vast a scale. It knew nothing of the variety of guilds of the "men of tools" clustered on the outskirts of the palace or settled in the villages to carry out the royal orders.

With the collapse of the Mycenaean empire, the palace-centered system was completely destroyed, never to be revived. The term *wanax* disappeared from the strictly political vocabulary. In its technical sense, to designate the royal function, it was replaced by the word *basileus,* whose strictly local meaning we have noted, and which in the plural designated not a single person who concentrated all forms of power in himself, but rather a category of notables who as a group occupied the highest reaches of the social hierarchy. With the rule of the *wanax* abolished, we find no more traces of an authority organized by the king, of an adminstrative apparatus, of a class of scribes. Writing itself disappeared, as though engulfed in the ruins of the palaces. When the Greeks rediscovered it toward the end of the ninth century, this time through borrowing from the Phoenicians, it was not only another type of script—a phonetic one—but a radically different cultural factor: no longer the specialty of a class of scribes, but an element of a common culture. Its social and psychological significance were also transformed—one might say reversed. The purpose of writing was no longer the production of archives for the king's private use within the palace. Now it served a public purpose: it allowed the various aspects of social and political life to be disclosed to the gaze of all people equally.

CHAPTER THREE

The Crisis of Sovereignty

The collapse of Mycenaean power and the spread of the Dorians throughout the Peloponnesos, into Crete, and as far as Rhodes inaugurated a new age for Greek civilization. The metallurgy of iron succeeded that of bronze. Cremation of the dead to a large extent replaced underground burial. Pottery changed radically as the depiction of animal and plant forms was abandoned in favor of geometrical decoration. Sharp separation of the parts of the vase, reduction of forms to the simplest outlines, adherence to a principle of spareness and severity that excluded the mystical elements of the Aegean tradition—such were the features of the new Geometric style. T. B. L. Webster goes so far as to speak of an actual revolution.[1] In this art, stripped to the bare essentials, he identifies an attitude of mind that he finds equally conspicuous in the other innovations of the period. By then people had become aware of a past distinct from the present: the Bronze Age, the heroic age, in contrast to the

[1] T. B. L. Webster, *From Mycenae to Homer* (London, 1958).

new era, dedicated to iron. The world of the dead was remote, cut off from that of the living; cremation had severed the earthly ties of the deceased. An unbridgeable distance had opened between humans and the gods: the figure of the god-king had vanished. Thus in every sphere a stricter demarcation of the different planes of reality prepared the way for the work of Homer—that epic poetry which tends to banish mystery even from religion.

In this chapter I wish especially to draw attention to the scope of the social transformations that had the most immediate repercussions on the structure of thought. It is language that first gives evidence of these transformations. From Mycenae to Homer, the vocabularies of ranks and titles, civil and military functions, and land tenure all but fell apart. The few terms that remained, such as *basileus* and *temenos*, no longer had exactly the same meanings now that the old system had been destroyed. Does this mean that there was no continuity between the Mycenaean and Homeric worlds? Is no comparison possible? Such a claim has been made.[2] Yet the picture of a small kingdom such as Ithaca, with its *basileus*, its assembly, its unruly nobles, and in the background its silent *demos* [common people], manifestly continues and sheds light on certain aspects of Mycenaean reality, however provincial and marginal to the palace they may be. The disappearance of the *wanax* seems to have left in place, side by side, the two social forces with which his power had had to come to terms: on the one hand the village

[2]See especially M. I. Finley, "Homer and Mycenae: Property and Tenure," *Historia*, 6 (1957), 133–159.

communities, on the other a warrior aristocracy whose most important families also held certain religious monopolies as a privilege of *genos* [lineage]. The search for a balance and accommodation between these opposing forces, set loose by the collapse of the palace-centered system and occasionally coming into violent confrontation, gave rise in a time of troubles to moral thought and political speculation that amounted to an early form of human "wisdom." This *sophia* appeared as early as the dawn of the seventh century, and was associated with a rather odd assortment of figures who came to be clothed with an almost legendary radiance and whom the Greeks continued to revere as their first true sages. *Sophia* was concerned not with the universe of *physis* [nature] but with the human world: the elements that made it up, the forces that divided it against itself, and the means by which they might be harmonized and unified so that their conflict might give birth to the human order of the city. This early wisdom was the fruit of a long history, difficult and harsh, in which many factors were interwoven, but which from the start turned from the Mycenaean concept of the sovereign to seek another path. The problems of power, of the forms it took and the factors that formed its substance, were immediately posed in new terms.

Indeed, it is not enough to say that during this period royalty was stripped of its prerogatives in Greece, and that even where it survived it had in fact given way to government by an aristocracy; we must add that the new *basileia* was no longer the Mycenaean royalty. The kingship had changed not only in name but in character. Neither in mainland Greece nor in Ionia, where a new wave of colonists in flight from the Dorian invasion had begun to settle, is any trace of a royal power of the Mycenaean type to be found. Even if we assume that the independent city-states that joined together in the Ionian League in the sixth century perpetuated an older organization in which local kings acknowledged the overlordship of a dynasty that ruled at Ephesus,[3] its supremacy would be analogous to that exercised by Agamemnon, in the *Iliad*, over kings who were his peers and who were subordinated to him only during a campaign conducted jointly under his leadership. Quite different, obviously, is the supervision imposed at every moment, over every person, every action, every thing, by the Mycenaean *wanax* through the agency of the palace.

With respect to Athens, the one place in all of Greece whose continuity with the Mycenaean era had not been brutally disrupted, Aristotle drew from the tradition of the Atthidographers [local historians of Attica] an account of the stages of what may be called the breakup of sovereignty.[4] The presence of the polemarch at the king's side as chief of the armed forces indicates that the sovereign had already lost his military function. The institution of the archon, which Aristotle says was established under the Codridae—in other words, as soon as the Achaeans from Pylos and the Peloponnesos who had taken refuge in Attica embarked for Ionia—marks a more decisive split. Once the notion of *arche,* command, had been severed from *basileia,* it became independent and deter-

[3]See Michel B. Sakellariou, *La migration grecque en Ionie* (Athens, 1958).

[4]Aristotle, *The Athenian Constitution*, III, 2–4; see Chester G. Starr, "The Decline of the Early Greek Kings," *Historia,* 10 (1961), 129–138.

mined the province of a strictly political reality. Elected first for a period of ten years, the archons were later replaced every year. The election system, even though it kept or borrowed some features of a religious proceeding, implied a new conception of power: *arche* was delegated every year by a human decision, through a choice that presupposed confrontation and discussion. This stricter delimitation of political power, which took the form of civic office, was complemented by *basileia*, which was now relegated to a specifically religious sphere. The *basileus* was no longer a quasi-divine person whose power was manifest at all levels; his responsibility was limited to certain priestly functions.

The image of the king as lord over all power was replaced by the idea of specialized social functions, each different from the other, whose adjustment posed difficult problems of equilibrium. The Athenian royal legends are significant here. They illustrate a theme very different from that found in many Indo-European myths of sovereignty.[5] To take a characteristic example, the Scythian royal legends, as reported by Herodotus, present the sovereign as a person above and beyond the various functional classes that made up society; since he represented them all, and since all equally found in him the source of the virtues by which they defined themselves, he no longer belonged to any one of them.[6] The

[5]On the problems of sovereignty at the human level—the king's relations with the various classes and the social group as a whole—see the observations of Georges Dumézil, "Religion indo-européenne: Examen de quelques critiques récentes," *Revue de l'Histoire des Religions*, 152 (1957), 8–30.

[6]Herodotus, IV, 5–6. See E. Benveniste, "Traditions indo-iraniennes

prototypical golden objects—the libation cup, the war ax, the plow (composed of share and yoke)—symbolized the three Scythian social categories: priest, soldier, and farmer. The king alone possessed all three at once. The human activities that were set against each other in society were integrated and made one in the person of the sovereign. The Athenian legends, on the other hand, were concerned with an inverse process: a crisis of succession which, instead of being settled by the victory of one claimant over the others and the concentration of all *arche* in his hands, led to a division of sovereignty, each claimant appropriating to himself one aspect of power and leaving the rest to his brothers. The emphasis was no longer on a single person who dominated social life, but on a multiplicity of functions that opposed each other and thus called for a reciprocal apportionment and delimitation.

On the death of Pandion, his two sons divided the paternal heritage between them. Erechtheus received the *basileia*; to Butes, married to Chthonia, his brother's daughter, went the *hierosyne* or priesthood. The *basileia* of Erechtheus rested on military power: Erechtheus was a fighter, the inventor of the chariot, and he was killed in battle. This first division failed to settle the dynastic problem. Erechtheus in turn left three sons—Cecrops, Me-

---

sur les classes sociales," *Journal asiatique*, 230 (1938), 529–549; G. Dumézil, *L'idéologie tripartie des Indo-européens* (Brussels, 1958), pp. 9–10; "Les trois 'trésors des ancêtres' dans l'épopée Narte," *Revue de l'Histoire des Religions*, 157 (1960), 141–154. We find an analogous theme in the royal legend of Orchomenus; see F. Vian, "La triade des rois d'Orchomène: Eteoclès, Phlegyas, Minyas," in *Hommage à Georges Dumèzil*, *Latomus*, 45, 215–224.

tion, and Pandorus. Beginning with the two elder, who founded rival lines, the contest for the throne recurred from generation to generation down to Aegeus, though without interrupting a continuous cycle of intermarriages between the two branches of the family. As H. Jeanmaire has shown, the struggle between the Cecropidae and the Metionidae expressed the tension of two opposing aspects of *basileia* itself.[7] If the episode is seen in the context of the entire tale of succession, the dynastic crisis reveals four concurrent principles at work within the sovereignty: a specifically religious principle, identified with Butes; a principle of military force, identified with Erechtheus, the Cecropidae, and Aegeus (who divided the *arche* into four parts, keeping the whole *kratos* [sovereignty] for himself); a principle connected with the soil and its virtues, identified with Chthonia and Pandorus (who brings us close to Pandora); and a principle of magical power, personified by the goddess Metis, wife of Zeus. This magical power applied particularly to the arts that made use of fire, which were under the protection of Hephaestus and Athena, gods of *metis* [craft] and patrons of artisans. It is tempting to compare these four principles with the four Ionian tribes, which may have had—and to which the Greeks explicitly gave—a functional distinction.[8]

[7]H. Jeanmaire, "La naissance d'Athéna et la royauté magique de Zeus," *Revue archéologique*, 48 (1956), 12–40.

[8]The four Ionian tribes are called Hopletes, Argadeis, Geleontes, and Aigikoreis, which H. Jeanmaire translates as warriors, artisans, royalty (with a religious function), and husbandmen (*Couroi et courètes* [Lille, 1959]). For a contrary view, see M. P. Nilsson, *Cults, Myths, Oracles, and Politics in Ancient Greece* (Lund, 1951), app. 1: "The Ionian Phylae"; see also G. Dumézil, "Métiers et classes fonctionnelles chez

What the myth suggests in its tale of conflict among brothers was systematically set forth by history and political theory, which presented the social body as a compound of heterogeneous elements, of separate parts (*moirai* or *mere*), of classes that had exclusive functions but were nevertheless expected to blend and coalesce.[9]

With the disappearance of the *wanax*, who by superhuman power had unified and given order to the diverse groups that made up the kingdom, new problems emerged. How was order to arise out of discord between rival groups and the clash of conflicting prerogatives and functions? How could a common life be founded on disparate elements? Or to apply the Orphics' formula, how, on the social level, could one emerge from many and many from one?[10]

The spirit of conflict and the spirit of union—Eris-Philia: these two divine entities, opposed and complementary, marked the two poles of society in the aristocratic world that followed the ancient kingships. An exaltation of the values of struggle, competition, and

---

divers peuples indo-européens," *Annales: Economies, Sociétés, Civilisations*, 1958, pp. 716-724.

[9]In particular Aristotle, *Politics*, II, 1261a.

[10]V. Ehrenberg notes that a basic contradiction lies at the heart of the Greek conception of society: the state is one and homogeneous; the human group is made up of multiple and heterogeneous parts. This contradiction remains implicit and unformulated, because the Greeks never made a clear distinction between state and society, or between the political and social levels. Hence the difficulty, not to say the confusion, of an Aristotle when he deals with the unity and plurality of the *polis* (V. Ehrenberg, *The Greek State* [Oxford, 1960], p. 89). This problem of the one and the many, implicit in social practice and expressed in some religious contexts, would be rigorously formulated only at the level of philosophical thought.

rivalry was associated with the sense of belonging to a single community, with its demands for social unity and cohesion. The spirit of *agon* [competition] that animated the *gene* [families] of the nobility was manifest in every sphere. Above all it was manifest in war. The chariot was gone, with everything it implied in the way of political and administrative centralization, but the horse continued to guarantee special military qualifications to its owner: the *hippeis* and *hippobotes* were at once members of a military elite and of a landed aristocracy. The image of the horseman linked skill in combat, high birth, wealth in land, and the right to take part in political life. The same competitiveness is found in the religious sphere: each *genos* asserted its rights to certain rituals, its possession of formulas, of secret chronicles, of divine symbols that were especially efficacious, which entitled it to powers and titles of authority. Finally, the entire sphere of protolaw, which governed the relations between families, itself constituted a sort of *agon*—a codified and regulated competition between opposing groups, a test of strength between *gene* comparable to the pitting of athletes against each other in the Games. Indeed, politics, too, had the form of *agon*: an oratorical contest, a battle of arguments whose theater was the agora, the public square, which had been a meeting place before it was a marketplace.[11] Those who contended with words, who opposed speech with speech, became in this hierarchical society a class of equals. As Hesiod would later

[11] The term harks back to the gathering of warriors, the *laos* joined in military formation. There appears to be an unbroken line of development from the early martial gathering to the gathering of citizens in the oligarchic states to the democratic *ecclesia*.

observe, all rivalry, all *eris* presupposes a relationship of equality: competition can take place only among peers.[12] This egalitarian spirit at the very heart of an agonistic conception of social life is a distinguishing feature of the outlook of the Greek warrior-aristocrats, and it played a part in casting the idea of power in new terms. *Arche* could no longer be the exclusive property of any one person. The state itself was shorn of all private and personal character; having escaped the jurisdiction of the *gene*, it came to be everybody's business.

The terms a Greek would use to express this concept are striking: he would say that certain deliberations, certain decisions must be brought *es to koinon* [to the commons], that the ancient privileges of the king and *arche* itself were set down *es to meson*, in the middle, at the center. The recourse to a spatial image to express the self-awareness that a human group has acquired, its sense of existing as a political unit, is of value not only as a comparison; it also reflects the creation of a social space that was altogether new. Indeed, urban buildings were no longer grouped, as before, about a royal palace ringed by fortifications. The city was now centered on the agora, the communal space and seat of the *hestia koine* [the central or public hearth], a public area where problems of general interest were debated. The city itself was now surrounded by walls, protecting and delineating the entire human group of which it was composed. On the spot where the royal citadel once rose—a private and privileged dwelling—the city erected temples that were open to public worship. On the ruins of the palace, on

---

[12]Hesiod, *Works and Days*, 25-26.

that acropolis which was henceforth consecrated to its gods, the community itself was now projected on the sacred plane, just as at the profane level it found its proper place in the expanse of the agora. What this urban framework in fact defined was a mental space; it opened up a new spiritual horizon. Once the city was centered on the public square, it was already a *polis* in every sense of the word.

CHAPTER FOUR

The Spiritual Universe of the *Polis*

The advent of the *polis* constitutes a decisive event in the history of Greek thought. Certainly, on the intellectual as well as the institutional level, the *polis* went through a number of stages and a variety of forms, and only in due time did all of its consequences become known. From the very outset, however, which we can place between the eighth and seventh centuries, it marked a departure, a genuine innovation. With the *polis*, social life and human relations took on a new form, and the Greeks were fully aware of its originality.[1]

The system of the *polis* implied, first of all, the extraordinary preeminence of speech over all other instruments of power. Speech became the political tool par excellence, the key to all authority in the state, the means of commanding and dominating others. This power of speech—which the Greeks made into a divinity, Peitho, the force of persuasion—brings to mind the efficacy of

[1]See V. Ehrenberg, "When Did the Polis Rise?," *Journal of Hellenic Studies*, 57 (1937), 147–159; "Origins of Democracy," *Historia*, 1 (1950), 519–548.

words and formulas in certain religious rituals, or the value attributed to the "pronouncements" of the king when he rendered final *themis* [judgment]. Actually, however, we are dealing with quite a different matter. Speech was no longer the ritual word, the precise formula, but open debate, discussion, argument. It presupposed a public to which it was addressed, as to a judge whose ruling could not be appealed, who decided with hands upraised between the two parties who came before him. It was this purely human choice that measured the persuasive force of the two addresses, ensuring the victory of one speaker over his adversary.

All questions of general concern that the sovereign had to settle, and which marked out the domain of *arche* [sovereignty], were now submitted to the art of oratory and had to be resolved at the conclusion of a debate. They therefore had to be formulated as a discourse, poured into the mold of antithetical demonstrations and opposing arguments. There was thus a close connection, a reciprocal tie, between politics and *logos*. The art of politics became essentially the management of language; and *logos* from the beginning took on an awareness of itself, of its rules and its effectiveness, through its political function. Historically, rhetoric and sophistry, by analyzing the forms of discourse as the means of winning the contest in the assembly and the tribunal, opened the way for Aristotle's inquiries, which in turn defined the rules of proof along with the technique of persuasion, and thus laid down a logic of the verifiably true, a matter of theoretical understanding, as opposed to the logic of the apparent or probable, which presided over the hazardous debates on practical questions.

A second feature of the *polis* was the full exposure given to the most important aspects of social life. We can even say that the *polis* existed only to the extent that a *public* domain had emerged, in each of the two differing but interdependent meanings of the term: an area of common interest, as opposed to private concerns, and open practices openly arrived at, as opposed to secret procedures. This insistence on openness led to the progressive appropriation by the group of the conduct, knowledge, and procedures that originally were the exclusive prerogatives of the *basileus*, or of the *gene* that held *arche*, and their exposure to public view. On the intellectual level, this double impulse toward democratization and disclosure had decisive consequences. Greek culture took form by opening to an ever widening circle—and finally to the entire *demos* [community]—access to the spiritual world reserved initially for an aristocracy of priests and warriors. (The Homeric epic is an early example of that process: from court poetry, sung first in the halls of the palace, it was freed, expanded, and transformed into a poetry for popular festivals.) But this broadening involved a radical transformation. Knowledge, values, and mental techniques, in becoming elements of a common culture, were themselves brought to public view and submitted to criticism and controversy. They were no longer preserved in family traditions as private tokens of power, and their exposure to public scrutiny fostered exegeses, varying interpretations, controversies, and impassioned debates. Now discussion, debate, polemic became the rules of the intellectual as well as the political game. The community's inexorable control was exercised over the creations of the mind no less than over the operations of the state. The law of the *polis*, as distinguished from the absolute power of the monarch, required that both be equally subject to a "rendering of accounts," *euthunai.* They could no longer be imposed by the authority of personal or religious prestige; they had to demonstrate their validity by processes of a dialectical sort.

Speech became the instrument of the city's political life; on the strictly intellectual level, writing became the medium of a common culture and permitted the complete dissemination of knowledge previously restricted or forbidden. Borrowed from the Phoenicians and modified to permit more precise transcription of Greek sounds, writing was able to fulfill this function of communication because it had become almost as widely known and used among citizens as the spoken language. The oldest known inscriptions in the Greek alphabet show that from the eighth century onward it was no longer a matter of specialized knowledge, reserved for scribes, but a technique in general use, freely diffused among the public.[2] Along with recitation from memory of texts by Homer and Hesiod—which remained traditional—writing constituted the basic element of Greek *paideia* [education].

Thus we can understand the significance of a demand that arose with the birth of the city: the writing down of the laws. Setting them down not only ensured their per-

[2]John Forsdyke, *Greece before Homer: Ancient Chronology and Mythology* (London, 1956), pp. 18ff.; see also the remarks of C. Preaux, "Du linéaire B créto-mycénien aux ostraca grecs d'Egypte," *Chronique d'Egypte,* 34 (1959), 79–85.

manence and stability; it also removed them from the private authority of the *basileis*, whose function was to "speak" the law. Thus they became public property, general rules that could be applied equally to all. In Hesiod's world, before the rise of the city, *dike* [justice] still operated on two levels, as though divided between heaven and earth. Here below, at the level of the small Boeotian farmer, *dike* was a determination of fact subject to the whim of kings, "devourers of gifts." In heaven it was a sovereign divinity, remote and inaccessible. But as a result of the public exposure provided by the written word, *dike*—without ceasing to be regarded as an ideal value—could be incarnated on a strictly human level. It could emerge as the law, a principle at once common to all and superior to all, a rational standard that was subject to discussion and modification by decree but which nevertheless expressed an order that was understood to be sacred.

Individuals who decided to make their knowledge public by means of writing did so either in the form of books, such as those that Anaximander and Pherecydes are said to have been the first to write, or those that Heraclitus deposited in the temple of Artemis at Ephesus, or in the form of *parapegmata*, monumental inscriptions on stone similar to those on which the city engraved the names of its magistrates or its priests (private citizens recorded astronomical observations or chronological tables based on them). Their ambition was not to make a display of their own discoveries or opinions; in setting forth such a message *es to meson*, they wished to make it the common property of the city, a standard that would,

53

like the law, be applicable to all.[3] Thus disclosed, their wisdom would take on a new consistency and objectivity: it would become the truth. We are no longer dealing with a religious secret, reserved for some few elect who had been favored by divine grace. Certainly the truth of the sage, like the religious secret, revealed what was fundamental, unveiled a higher reality that far transcended the mass of humanity; but in being committed to writing, it was wrenched from the closed circle of the cults and displayed in broad daylight before the gaze of the whole city. Those who wrote thus recognized that their message was within the reach of all by right, and agreed to submit it, like political debate, to the judgment of all, in the hope that in the end all would acknowledge and accept it.

This transformation of secret wisdom into a body of public truths has a parallel in another area of social experience. The early priesthoods, which belonged to certain *gene* of their own and claimed special intimacy with a divine power, were appropriated by the *polis* for its own uses, once it had become established, and turned into official city cults. The protection that the deity had formerly reserved for his favorites would henceforth be extended to the entire community. But to speak of a city cult is to speak of a public cult. All the old *sacra*, badges of investiture, religious symbols, emblems, *xoana* [wooden images], jealously preserved as talismans of power in the privacy of palaces or the crannies of priestly houses, now moved to the temple, an open and public place. Within that impersonal space, which faced outward and which

[3]See Diogenes Laertius, I, 43; letter from Thales to Pherecydes.

now projected the decoration of its sculptured friezes toward the outside, the old idols were in turn transformed. Along with their hidden character, they lost their quality as efficacious symbols and became simply "images," with no ritual function other than to be seen, no religious meaning other than their appearance. Of the large cult statue lodged in the temple to represent the god, one could say that all its *esse* [being] now consisted of a *percipi* [perception]. The *sacra,* formerly charged with a dangerous power and withheld from public view, became a spectacle in full view of the city, a "lesson on the gods," just as the secret chronicles and occult formulas shed their mystery and their religious force to become the "truths" debated by the sages in full view of the city.

Still, it was by no means without difficulty or resistance that social life was thus brought into full public view. The process of disclosure occurred by stages; in every area it met with obstacles that limited its progress. Even in the high classical period, secret governmental practices preserved a form of power that worked in mysterious ways and by supernatural means. The Spartan regime offers the best examples of these hidden procedures, but the use of hidden sanctuaries as tools of government, private oracles reserved exclusively for certain officials, and undisclosed handbooks of divination kept by certain leaders is equally well attested elsewhere. In addition, many cities entrusted their survival to the possession of secret relics: the remains of the hero, whose tomb could be revealed to no one, on pain of destroying the state, save to those officials who alone were qualified to receive such dangerous information when they took office. The political value attributed to these secret talismans was not simply a survival of the past. It answered definite social needs. Did not the city's safety necessarily set in motion forces that eluded the calculations of human reason, elements that could not be appraised in debate or foreseen at the close of deliberation? This intervention of a supernatural power whose role was ultimately decisive—Herodotus' Fate, Thucydides' *Tyche* [Chance]—must be taken into account and given its place in the political system. Public worship of the Olympian gods could answer to that function only in part. That worship had to do with a divine world that was too general and too remote; it defined a sacred order that was exactly the opposite of the secular sphere where the city's administration was located, as the *hieros* [sacred] was opposed to the *hosios* [secular]. The desacralization of an entire plane of political life had as its counterpart an official religion that kept human affairs at arm's length and was no longer directly involved in the vicissitudes of *arche.* Yet however clear-sighted the political leaders and however wise the citizens, the assembly's decisions bore on a future that remained fundamentally opaque and which the intelligence could not altogether grasp. So it became essential to ensure as much control over that future as possible by other means—means that called into effect no human abilities, but rather the power of ritual. The political "rationalism" that presided over the city's institutions was certainly in sharp contrast to the old religious procedures of government, but still it never went so far as to abolish them. [4]

[4]The role of divination in the political life of the Greeks comes to

In the religious sphere, moreover, associations based on secrecy developed at the fringes of the city and alongside the public cult. Sects, brotherhoods, and mysteries were closed groups, with hierarchies of ranks and degrees, modeled on the initiation societies. Their function was to single out, through a series of ordeals, an elect minority who would enjoy privileges not available to the mass of people. But in contrast to the initiations to which the young warriors, the *kouroi,* had once been subjected and which conferred power upon them, the new secret groups were confined to a purely religious sphere. In the framework of the city, initiation could now bring only a "spiritual" transformation, with no political connotations. The elect, the *epoptai,* were the unsullied, the saints. Akin to the divine, they were indeed dedicated to a special destiny, but they would meet it in the hereafter. The preferment they would gain belonged to another world.

The mysteries offered to all those who wished to undergo initiation, with no restriction of birth or rank, the promise of a blissful immortality that had once been an exclusively royal privilege; they disclosed to the wider circle of the initiated the religious secrets that had been the sole property of such priestly families as the Kerykes and the Eumolpides. But despite this democra-

---

mind. In general, it may be noted that every civic office still had a sacred character. But it was the same with politics as with the judiciary. In the legal framework the religious practices that originally had value in themselves became a prologue to the hearing of each case. Similarly, the rites to which civic officers still submitted on taking office, such as sacrifice and oath taking, constituted the formal structure and no longer the internal strength of political life. In this sense, there was indeed secularization.

tization of religious privilege, the mysteries were never revealed to the public. On the contrary, what defined them as mysteries was their claim to attain to a truth that was inaccessible by any normal route and which was not to be "exposed" in any way, to gain a revelation so exceptional that it gave access to a religious life unknown to the state religion and reserved for the initiated a destiny that had nothing in common with the ordinary condition of citizens. Thus secrecy, in contrast to the public character of the official cult, acquired a special religious significance: it defined a religion of personal salvation whose goal was to transform the individual independently of the social order, to bring about in him, as it were, a new birth that would pluck him from the mass of people and permit him to reach a different plane of life.

But in that same area, the inquiries of the earliest sages were proceeding to overtake the preoccupations of the religious groups until they sometimes merged with them. Their teachings, like the revelations of the mysteries, claimed to transform the individual from within, to lift him to a higher state, to make of him a unique being, almost a god—a *theios aner* [godlike man]. When the city fell victim to disorder and pollution and turned to such a sage to ask the way out of its difficulties, it did so precisely because he seemed a being apart and exceptional, a holy man isolated and removed to the fringes of the community by his whole manner of life. Conversely, when a sage addressed himself to the city, in speech or in writing, it was always to transmit a truth that came from above, and which even after its disclosure did not cease to belong to another world, one alien to ordinary life. The early wisdom thus took form as a sort of contradiction that arose from its paradoxical nature: it divulged to the public a knowledge that it proclaimed at the same time to be unavailable to the majority. Was not its purpose to unveil the unseen, to make visible the world of the *adela* [unknown] that hid behind appearances? Wisdom revealed a truth so marvelous that it could be won only at the cost of painful effort—so marvelous that it remained, like the vision of the *epoptai*, hidden from the eyes of the common people. To be sure, the secret had to be formulated in words—but the mass of people could not grasp its meaning. Wisdom brought the mystery out into the public square; it examined it and studied it, and still it did not altogether cease to be a mystery. For the traditional initiation rites that guarded access to the forbidden revelations, *sophia* or *philosophia* substituted other ordeals: a rule of life, a road of *askesis* [training], a path of inquiry that—along with the methods of discussion and argumentation, or the new mental tools such as mathematics—preserved the ancient divinatory practices and spiritual exercises aimed at concentration, ecstasy, and the separation of the spirit from the body.

From its birth, then, philosophy was to find itself in an ambiguous position. In its inspiration and its development it was related to both the initiations into the mysteries and the disputations of the agora; it wavered between the sense of secrecy peculiar to the cults and the public argument that characterized political activity. Depending on the place, the time, and the trend, it might, like the Pythagorean sect in sixth-century Magna Graecia [southern Italy], be organized in a closed brotherhood that refused to entrust a purely esoteric doctrine to writing; or it might, like the Sophistic movement, become completely integrated with public life, presented as a preparation for the exercise of power in the city and offered freely to any citizen by means of lessons paid for in cash. Greek philosophy perhaps never completely extricated itself from the ambiguity of its origins. The philosopher would continually waver between two attitudes, hesitate between two conflicting temptations. At times he would claim that he alone was qualified to direct the state; arrogantly taking the place of the god-king, he would take it upon himself, in the name of the "knowledge" that elevated him above ordinary men, to reform all social life and rule the city as its sovereign authority. At other times he would withdraw from the world to immerse himself in a purely private wisdom; gathering about him a few disciples, he would set out with them to establish his own city within a city. Turning his back on public life, he would seek salvation in learning and contemplation.

To the two aspects I have indicated—the magic spell of the spoken word and the increasingly public conduct of affairs—another feature was added to mark the spiritual universe of the *polis*. Those who made up the city, however different in origin, rank, and function, appeared somehow to be "like" one another. This likeness laid the foundation for the unity of the *polis*, since for the Greeks only those who were alike could be mutually united by *philia*, joined in the same community. In the framework of the city, the tie that bound one man to another thus became a reciprocal relationship, replacing the hierarchical relations of submission and dominance. All those who shared in the state were defined as *homoioi*—men who were alike—and later more abstractly as *isoi*, or equals. Despite everything that might set them at odds with one another in the day-to-day business of social life, on the political level the citizens conceived of themselves as interchangeable units within a system whose law was the balance of power and whose norm was equality. In the sixth century this image of the human world was precisely expressed in the concept of *isonomia*—that is, the equal participation of all citizens in the exercise of power. But before it had acquired this fully democratic meaning, and before it had inspired such institutional reforms as those of Cleisthenes, the ideal of *isonomia* was able to convey or to extend communal aspirations that went back to the very origins of the *polis*. There is some evidence that the terms *isonomia* and *isocratia* served in aristocratic circles to define an oligarchical regime that contrasted with the absolute power of one man (the *monarchia* or *tyrannis*). In this regime, *arche* was reserved for a small number to the exclusion of the majority, but was divided equally among all members of that elite group.[5] That the requirement of *isonomia* was able to acquire such strength by the end of the sixth century, that it could justify the popular demand for ready access by the *demos* to all civic offices, may no doubt be explained by the fact that it was rooted in a very old egalitarian tradition, and even responded to certain psychological

[5]V. Ehrenberg, in "Origins of Democracy," recalls that the song of Harmodius and Aristogiton honors the *eupatridai* for having made the Athenians *isonomous*; see also Thucydides, III, 62.

attitudes of the aristocracy of the *hippeis*. It was in fact this mounted military nobility that first established a correspondence between martial qualifications and the right to participate in public affairs—a correspondence that was never again questioned. In the *polis* the status of the soldier coincided with that of the citizen: anyone who had a place in the city's military structure had by the same token a place in its political organization. But after the middle of the seventh century, modifications in equipment and a revolution in combat technology transformed the figure of the warrior, completely altering his social status and his psychological makeup.[6]

The appearance of the hoplite, a heavily armed line soldier, and his use in close formation on the principle of the phalanx, struck a decisive blow to the military prerogatives of the *hippeis*. All those who could bear the costs of their hoplite equipment—that is, the small free landowners who made up the *demos*, such as the *zeugitai* in Athens—were assigned to the same level as those who owned horses. But here, too, the democratization of the military function—formerly an aristocratic privilege—entailed a complete reshaping of the warrior ethic. The Homeric hero, the stalwart charioteer, might still live on in the figure of the *hippeus*; he no longer had much in common with this citizen-soldier, the hoplite. What counted for the *hippeus* was the individual exploit, splendid performance in single combat. In battle, a

---

[6]See A. Andrews, *The Greek Tyrants* (London, 1956), chap. 3, "The Military Factor"; F. E. Adcock, *The Greek and Macedonian Art of War* (Berkeley and Los Angeles, 1957); on dating the appearance of the hoplite, see P. Courbin, "Une tombe géométrique d'Argos," *Bulletin de Correspondance hellénique*, 81 (1957), 322–384.

mosaic of face-to-face duels between *promachoi* [champions], military worth was asserted in the form of an *aristeia*, a wholly personal superiority. The warrior found the boldness that enabled him to perform such brilliant feats of arms in a sort of exaltation or warlike frenzy, *lyssa*, into which he was thrown, as though beside himself, by *menos*, the ardor inspired by a god. But the hoplite no longer engaged in individual combat; if he felt the temptation to engage in a purely individual act of valor, he was obliged to resist it. He was the man of elbow-to-elbow warfare, of shoulder-to-shoulder struggle. He was trained to hold ranks, to march in formation, to throw himself directly against the enemy, to take care not to leave his position at the height of battle. Martial virtue, then, no longer had anything to do with *thymos*, but consisted in *sophrosyne*—a complete mastery of self, a constant striving to submit oneself to a common discipline, the coolness necessary to restrain those instinctive pressures that would risk upsetting the discipline of the formation as a whole. The phalanx made of the hoplite, as the city made of the citizen, an interchangeable unit, one element like all the others, and one whose *aristeia*, or individual worth, must never again be demonstrated except within the framework imposed by coordinated maneuvers, group cohesion, mass action—the new instruments of victory. Even in war, *eris*—the desire to overcome an adversary, to affirm one's superiority over another—must give way to *philia*, the spirit of community; the power of the individual must yield to the law of the group. When Herodotus mentions—as he does after each account of a battle—the names of the cities and the individuals who proved bravest at Plataea, he gives the

63

palm among the Spartans to Aristodemus, one of the three hundred Lacedaemonians who had defended Thermopylae, and who alone had returned safe and sound; anxious to clear himself of the opprobrium the Spartans attached to his survival, he sought and found death at Plataea in the performance of noble exploits. But it was not to him that the Spartans awarded the funeral honors that were bestowed only on the very best, as the prize of bravery; they denied him the *aristeia* because, fighting in fury like a man deranged by *lyssa*, he had broken rank.[7]

This account strikingly illustrates a psychological attitude that is evident not only in the realm of warfare but on all levels of social life, an attitude that marked a decisive turning point in the history of the *polis*. There came a time when the city rejected the traditional modes of aristocratic behavior, which tended to exalt the prestige of individuals and of *gene*, reinforce their power, and raise them above the mass. Thus it condemned as excess, as *hybris*—in the same category as martial frenzy and the pursuit of purely personal glory in combat—the display of wealth , costly garments, magnificent funerals, excessive displays of grief in mourning, behavior that was too flamboyant in women or too confident and bold in aristocratic youths.

All these practices were now rejected because, by accentuating social inequalities and the sense of distance between individuals, they aroused envy, produced discord within the group, threatened its equilibrium and cohesion, and divided the city against itself. What was

[7]Herodotus, IX, 71.

now extolled was an austere ideal of reserve and re-straint, a severe, almost ascetic way of life that obscured differences of manner and rank between citizens in order to bring them closer together, to unite them like the members of one big family.

In Sparta the military seems almost certainly to have played the decisive role in the advent of the new mentality. The Sparta of the seventh century was not yet the state whose originality would call forth in the other Greeks an admiration mixed with shock. At that time it was caught up in the general movement that was carrying the aristocracies of the various cities toward extravagance, causing them to wish for a more refined existence and to seek out profitable undertakings. The break came between the seventh and sixth centuries. Sparta turned in upon itself and became frozen in those institutions that dedicated it wholly to war. It not only repudiated the display of wealth, but closed itself off to all foreign contacts—no commerce, no craft activity. The use of precious metals was prohibited, and so was the use of gold and silver currency. Remaining outside the main intellectual currents, Sparta now neglected the arts and letters for which it had once been famous. Greek philosophy and thought therefore appear to owe it nothing.

But one can only say "appear." The social and political changes that the new techniques of warfare brought to Sparta and which turned it into a city of hoplites expressed at the institutional level the same demand for a balanced human world, regulated by law, which the sages were formulating on a strictly conceptual level elsewhere, in cities that were experiencing mutinies and domestic upheavals for want of a solution like the Spartans'. Scholars have rightly insisted on the archaism of those institutions to which Sparta adhered so obstinately: age groups, martial initiation rites, secret societies. But we must also stress other features that placed Sparta ahead of its time: the egalitarian spirit of a reform that abolished the ancient opposition between *laos* and *demos* in order to establish a corps of citizen-soldiers, defined as *homoioi*, each of whom in the beginning had a portion of land, a *kleros*, exactly equal to that of every other. To this first form of *isomoira* [equal shares] (perhaps later there was a second distribution of land) must be added the communal aspect of a social life that imposed the same austere regimen on everyone, which in its abhorrence of luxury codified even the way a private house was to be built, and which instituted the *syssitia*, communal meals for which each man furnished monthly his allotted portion of barley, wine, cheese, and figs. It must finally be noted that Sparta's regime, with its double royalty, the *apella* [assembly], the ephors, and the *gerousia* [council of elders], achieved an "equilibrium" among social elements that represented opposing duties, virtues, and values. On that reciprocal equilibrium was based the unity of the state, with each element kept by the others within limits it might not overstep. Plutarch thus assigned to the *gerousia* the function of a counterweight that maintained a continual balance between the popular *apella* and the royal authority, aligning itself now on the side of the kings to keep democracy in check, now on the side of the people to check the power of any one person.[8] In the same way, the institution of the ephors represented a

[8]Plutarch, "Life of Lycurgus," V, 11, and Aristotle, *Politics*, 1265b35.

martial element in the social body, "junior" and belonging to the people, in contrast to the aristocratic *gerousia*, whose "senior" traits of levelheadedness and wisdom were needed to counterbalance the martial daring and vigor of the *kouroi*.

In the Spartan state, society no longer formed a pyramid with the king at its apex, as in the Mycenaean kingdoms. All those who had submitted to military training and the series of tests and initiations it entailed, and thus had a *kleros* and took part in the *syssitia*, had been raised to the same level. That level was what defined the city.[9] The social order thus no longer appeared to depend on the sovereign; it was no longer bound to the inventive power of an exceptional individual, to his activity as an organizer. On the contrary, it was the social order that held the power of all individuals in check, setting limits on the urge to enlarge one's scope. The social order came first with respect to power. *Arche* in reality belonged exclusively to the law. Any individual or faction that tried to secure a monopoly on *arche* threatened the *homonoia* [unanimity] of the social body by such an attack on the balance of all other forces, and thereby put the city's very existence at risk.

But if the new Sparta thus acknowledged the supremacy of law and order, its purpose in doing so was to prepare for war: the reshaping of the state was above all a response to military preoccupations. The *homoioi* were more thoroughly drilled in the practice of battle than in

[9]Of course, alongside the citizens and in contrast to them, the city included all those who in varying degrees were denied the privileges of full citizenship: in Sparta, the *hypomeiones*, *perioikoi*, helots, and slaves. Equality stands out against a background of inequality.

the disputations of the agora. Thus in Sparta speech could never become the political tool it was elsewhere, or take shape as discussion, argumentation, rebuttal. In place of Peitho, the force of persuasion, as an instrument of the law, the Lacedaemonians extolled the power of Phobos, that fear which made all citizens bow in obedience. They boasted of relishing only brevity in speeches, and of preferring sententious and pithy turns of phrase to the subtleties of debate. For them speech was still *rhetrai*, those quasi-oracular laws to which they submitted without discussion and which they refused to expose to public scrutiny by writing them down. However advanced Sparta may have been, it left to others the honor of fully expressing the new conception of order, in which the city became a balanced and harmonious cosmos under the rule of law. It was not the Lacedaemonians that could define and explicate, in all their consequences, the moral and political ideas that they were among the first to embody in their institutions.

CHAPTER FIVE

The Crisis of the City: The Earliest Sages

In a dialogue now lost, *On Philosophy*, Aristotle evoked the great cataclysms that periodically destroy humankind, and traced the steps the scattered survivors and their descendants must take each time to reconstruct civilization. Those who escaped Deucalion's flood thus had first to rediscover the basic means of supporting life and then to reinvent the arts that enhance it. In a third stage, Aristotle went on, "they turned their attention to the organization of the *polis*; they invented laws and all the bonds that link the parts of a city together; and this invention they called Wisdom. Such was the wisdom (in advance of physical science, *physike theoria*, and of the supreme Wisdom that is concerned with divine realities) that was given to the Seven Sages, who invented the virtues suitable to a citizen."[1]

It would be idle to base any historical conclusions on the tradition of the Seven Sages. The list of the Seven is

---

[1]On Aristotle's *On Philosophy*, see A.-J. Festugière, *Le Dieu cosmique*, vol. 2 of *La révélation d'Hermès Trismégiste* (Paris, 1949), pp. 219ff. and App. 1.

69

shifting and variable; it flouts chronology and ignores probability. Nevertheless, the political and social role attributed to the sages and the maxims ascribed to them bring together some figures who otherwise are unlike in every way: a Thales, to whose many other abilities were added those of a statesman; a Solon, who besides being an elegiac poet and arbiter of Athenian political conflicts, rejected the opportunity to gain a tyranny; a Periander, who became tyrant of Corinth; an Epimenides, the very model of the inspired shaman or *theios aner*, living on mallow and asphodel, whose soul left his body at will. Out of a mixture of pure legend, historical allusions, and political and moral maxims, the more or less mythical tradition of the Seven Sages allows us to reach out and grasp a moment of social history—a moment of crisis that began at the end of the seventh century and unfolded in the sixth, a time of troubles in which we catch a glimpse of the economic conditions that gave rise to internal conflicts. On the religious and moral plane, the Greeks experienced this time as a questioning of their whole system of values, a blow to the very order of the world, a state of defect and defilement.

This crisis led to legal and social reforms that are associated specifically with such holy men as Epimenides as well as with such lawgivers as Solon, such mediators as Pittacus, and such tyrants as Periander. In the intellectual sphere, too, efforts were made to map out the framework and the fundamental concepts of a new Greek ethics. Simplifying matters greatly, we can say that the starting point of the crisis was economic; that initially it took the form of agitation that was both social and religious; but that, given the conditions peculiar to the city, it led finally to the birth of a moral and political thought that was secular, and which dealt with the problems of order and disorder in human society in a purely pragmatic fashion.

The economic transformations—which we can barely sketch here—were linked to a phenomenon that seems no less decisive on the cultural level: the resumption and development of contacts with the East, which had been broken off with the collapse of the Mycenaean empire. Relations between mainland Greece and the East were reestablished in the eighth century through Phoenician seamen. On the Ionian coast the Greeks began to deal with the Anatolian hinterland, particularly with Lydia. But in the last quarter of the seventh century the economies of European and Asian cities turned boldly outward. At that time sea traffic expanded beyond the eastern Mediterranean, which resumed its role as a pathway of communication. The trading area extended on the west as far as Africa and Spain, and on the east to the Black Sea.[2] This widening of the maritime horizon was also a response to an acute demand for grain created by population pressure—a problem made all the greater by the fact that Hellenic agriculture tended now to favor the more profitable cultivation of vineyards and olive groves,

[2]On the expansion of the Greeks throughout the Mediterranean and the resumption of contacts with the East, see Jean Bérard, *La colonisation grecque de l'Italie méridionale et de la Sicile dans l'antiquité* (Paris, 1957) and "La migration éolienne," *Revue archéologique* (1959), pp. 1-28; Thomas J. Dunbabin, *The Greeks and Their Eastern Neighbours: Studies in the Relations between Greece and the Countries of the Near East in the Eighth and Seventh Centuries* (London, 1957); Carl Roebuck, *Ionian Trade and Colonization* (New York, 1959); Michel B. Sakellariou, *La migration grecque en Ionie* (Athens, 1958).

whose products could be exported and traded. A search for land, for food, and for metal—such was the triple objective of Greek expansion across the Mediterranean. During the Dark Age, in a Greece isolated and without mineral wealth, gold and silver had become scarce, if they did not disappear altogether. In the eighth century new sources of precious metals opened up; throughout the seventh, the amount of gold, silver, and electrum put into circulation in the Greek world increased. Their expanded use took various forms: jewelry, the work of gold- and silversmiths, personal objects and votive offerings, wealth privately held or hoarded in temples; and finally, after its invention by the Lydian kings at the end of the seventh century, coinage.

It is not easy to appraise with any precision the changes in social structure that were brought about by the orientation of a whole sector of the Greek economy toward overseas trade. In the absence of direct evidence, we can only infer the nature and extent of those changes from literary testimony that indicates new forms of sensibility and thought. In this respect lyric poetry is a valuable source. It demonstrates that it was not only on pottery, in pictorial themes, and in ornamentation that the East left its mark. During the seventh century the tastes and manners of a Greek aristocracy that was attracted by luxury, refinement, and opulence were inspired by the ideal of *habrosyne*, of the magnificent and exquisite, which it found in the Oriental world.[3] From then on the display of wealth became an element in the prestige of

[3]See Santo Mazzarino, *Fra oriente e occidente: Ricerche di storia grecia arcaica* (Florence, 1947).

the *gene*; along with military prowess and religious qualifications, it was a means of indicating supremacy, of ensuring domination over rivals. And by becoming involved in the realm of wealth, the aristocratic *eris* introduced the ferment of alienation and division into Greek society. New figures emerged among the nobility: the wellborn man, the *kalos kagathos*, who engaged in maritime trade, either for love of money or out of need. A part of the aristocracy was transformed, passing, as Louis Gernet has written, from the "feudal" stage to that of "gentleman farmer."[4] We see the emergence of a type of landed proprietor who oversaw the yield of his lands, specialized in particular crops, and tried to increase his holdings by acquisition from the reserves that remained open to reclamation after the allotments to slaves and the *kleroi* of free smallholders. The nobleman, who was now also a man of wealth, extended his hold on the *eschatie* [outlying lands] at the expense of the village collectives, and could even appropriate the goods of those under obligation to him—dependents or potential debtors. The concentration of landed property in a very small number of hands and the subjugation of the greater part of the *demos*, reduced to the condition of "sixth-parters," made the agrarian problem the key issue of the Archaic period. No doubt a population of artisans developed, which must have been relatively numerous in certain fields, such as pottery and metalwork. (A technical fact of great significance must be noted in regard to metalwork: the replacement of bronze with iron for ob-

[4]L. Gernet, "Horoi," in *Studi in onore de U. E. Paoli* (Florence, 1955), p. 348.

jects in general use at the end of the eighth century.)
Artisans, together with tradesmen and all the people
along the coast and in port whose living came from the
sea, made up a new social category whose importance
would continue to grow—even in the city, the home of
the aristocracy. But in the seventh century, the revived
distinction between "urban" and "rural" meant that the
nobility—living *en astu*, in the city, where public buildings associated with *arche* were concentrated—had to
reckon again with a peasant class that provided them
with food and lived in the outlying villages, the *demoi*.

These technical and economic developments were
not limited to the Greek world; the Phoenician cities, in
the flush of commercial expansion since the ninth century, had experienced similar changes.[5] What was peculiar to Greece was the reaction those changes produced in
society: the refusal to accept a situation that was felt and
denounced as *anomia* [lawlessness] and the restructuring
of social life in its entirety to make it accord with communal and egalitarian aspirations. Those aspirations were
all the stronger because, with the coming of the Iron Age,
the powerful lost all decency, and *Aidos* [Shame] had to
flee the world for the heavens. With the way thus left clear
for the unleashing of individual passions and *hybris*, social relations were marked by violence, guile, despotism,
and injustice. The work of renewal went on at several
levels: it was simultaneously religious, legal, political,
and economic. Its constant aim was to curb the *dynamis* of

[5] On the similarities and differences between the Phoenician and
Greek worlds at the socioeconomic level, see the comments of
G. Thomson, *The First Philosophers*, vol. 2 of *Studies in Ancient Greek
Society* (London, 1955).

the *gene*, to set limits to their ambition, their enterprise, and their will to power, by subjecting them to a general rule whose constraints applied equally to all. This higher standard was the *dike* that was invoked by the sage as a divine power, that was promulgated by the lawgiver, and that might occasionally inspire tyrants, though they distorted it in imposing it by force. *Dike* was to establish a true equilibrium among citizens, a guarantee of *eunomia*: the equitable distribution of duties, honors, and power among the individuals and factions that made up the social body. *Dike* was thus to reconcile and harmonize these elements and make of them a single community, a unified city.

The first evidence of the new spirit has to do with certain legal matters. Legislation concerning homicide marks the moment when murder ceased to be a private affair, a settling of accounts between *gene*. Blood revenge, which had been limited to a narrow circle but had been obligatory for the relatives of the dead man, and thus could set in motion a disastrous cycle of murder and reprisal, was supplanted by repression organized by the city, controlled by the group, and involving the community as a whole. Now the murderer defiled not only the victim's relatives, but the entire community. This universalized condemnation of the crime, the horror henceforth aroused by every kind of murder, the haunting memory of *miasma* that bloodshed could evoke for a city or a region, the demand for an expiation that was at the same time a purging of evil—all these attitudes are connected with the religious awakening that took place throughout the country with the rise of Dionysiac religion, and which in some special settings took the form of a cult movement, such as that of the Orphics. This religious revival was characterized by teachings on what became of the soul, its punishment in Hades, the hereditary transmission of evil, the cycle of reincarnation, and the community of all animate beings, and by the establishment of purificatory rites in accord with the new beliefs. Plato, discussing homicide in the ninth book of the *Laws*, still felt the need to refer explicitly to the doctrine, the *logos*, of the "priests who attend to the *teletai* [Orphic rites]." In the line of these purifying sages, the figure of Epimenides stands out in particularly bold relief. Plutarch called him a sage in divine matters, with the *sophia* given to "the enraptured and the initiate"; it was he they called to Athens to drive off the *miasma* that had settled over the city after the slaughter of the Cylonians. He organized rituals of catharsis and was also an inspired soothsayer, whose knowledge, Aristotle tells us, disclosed the past rather than the future; indeed, his gift of second sight brought ancient transgressions into the open, disclosing hitherto unknown crimes, whose taint brought disturbance and disease to individuals and entire cities—the frenzied delirium of *mania* with its consequent disorder, violence, and murder. But this religious reformer, founder of sanctuaries and rituals, appears also as a political adviser whom Solon made a party to his legislative work. For at bottom the sage and the politician had the same aim: to set social life in order, to bring together and unify the city. In his life of Solon, Plutarch stresses Epimenides' role in the regulation of mourning, which he made calmer and more moderate, and in measures related to the proper conduct of women. "Most important of all," Plutarch concludes, "by sundry rites of propitiation and purification, and by sacred foundations, he hallowed and consecrated the city, and made it be observant of justice and more easily inclined" (let itself be more easily persuaded: *eupeithe*) "to unanimity" (*homonoia*).[6]

A brief but suggestive remark of Aristotle's allows us a better grasp of how, at such a turning point in the city's history, the religious, the judicial, and the social could find themselves allied in a common renewal effort.[7] Aristotle wished to show the inherent nature of the *polis*: that it was like an extended family, since it was formed by the merging of villages that themselves were a merger of households. He noted that the *oikos*, the domestic family, is a natural community, a *koinonia*, and recalled the names by which Charondas and Epimenides designated its members. The parallel is interesting in itself. Charondas was the lawgiver of Catana; like Zaleucus of Locris, who we are told was his master and with whom his name is frequently associated, he is said to have given his *Laws* a prelude similar to the one Plato gave his own ninth chapter, on criminal law. What we have here is a genuine incantation, an *epode*, which was to be sung and which was addressed to those whose minds were obsessed with thoughts of impious and criminal acts. Before decreeing repressive penalties, the legislators hoped to treat the wicked preventively with purifying magic, a sort of *goeteia*, which employed the soothing properties of words and music. The criminal was

[6]Plutarch, "The Life of Solon," XII, 7–12 [English translation by Bernadotte Perrin (New York and London: Loeb Classical Library, 1914)].

[7]Aristotle, *Politics*, 1252b15.

thought of as one "possessed," a creature driven mad by an evil *daimon*, the embodiment of an ancestral taint. The legislator's chanted *katharsis* restored health and well-being to this sick and troubled soul, in the same way that Epimenides' purifying rituals reestablished calm, moderation, and *homonoia* in a city overwhelmed by the dissension and violence brought on by past crimes.

But Aristotle's observation went further. Charondas and Epimenides referred to the members of the *oikos* by the terms *homosipuoi* and *homokapoi*, which emphasize a "similarity" between them, borne out by the fact that they shared the same bread, ate at the same table. This is precisely the state of mind that produced, as we have seen, the Spartan institution of *syssitia* between *homoioi*—a matter of giving citizens the feeling that in some way they were brothers. Nothing was more likely to strengthen this conviction than partaking of food prepared at the same hearth and shared at the same table: the meal became a communion that endowed companions at table with a common identity, a sort of consanguinity. From then on it was understood that the murder of a fellow citizen would provoke in the social body the same religious horror, the same feeling of sacrilege and defilement, that was aroused by a crime against a blood relative. Proof that a social conscience did indeed develop along these lines is to be found in the semantic evolution of *authentes*, the word for a murderer. First it denoted one who murdered his relative; then the murderer who was not a member of his victim's family, but who had some connection with that family, and so was branded by the same strong word that was applied to the murderer of his own kin, out of respect for the hatred and religious repulsion the victim's relatives felt toward him; and finally, the murderer of anyone at all, with no connotation of a special relationship with the victim's family. In the passage from private revenge to judicial punishment for the crime, the word that defined the murderer of a relative and then the murderer with some connection to the victim's relatives could continue to be used to designate the criminal with respect to all his fellow citizens.[8] Moreover, what was good and sufficient for crimes of blood was good and sufficient for other offenses as well. Aristotle and Plutarch counted among the happiest of Solon's innovations the principle that the wrong done to a particular individual is actually an attack on all; so Solon gave each person the right to intervene formally on behalf of anyone who had suffered an injury and to pursue *adikia* [injustice] although he was not himself the victim.

The various traits the Greeks assembled to form the figure of an Epimenides are no isolated piece of evidence. In the legendary tradition of Pythagoreanism the figure of Abaris appears with other sages—Aristeas, Hermotimus—not only as a shaman who flew through the air with his golden arrow, lived without food, and sent his soul forth to roam far from his body; he was also an interpreter of oracles, a religious reformer, and a purifier; he established new rituals of public worship (the Proerosia [a spring festival] at Athens); he opened sanctuaries for the community's protection (that of Kore the protectress at Sparta); he initiated purgation rites by

---

[8]See L. Gernet, *Droit et société dans la Grèce ancienne* (Paris, 1955), pp. 29–50. For a contrary view, see P. Chantraine, "Encore 'Αὐθέντης.'" in *Hommage à Μανόλη Τριανταφυλλίδη* (Athens, 1960), pp. 89–93.

which cities held off a *loimos* [plague]. A historical individual such as Onomacritus, associated with Musaeus, whose oracles he compiled—and falsified when necessary—took the part of soothsayer under the Pisistratids, collecting for their use a compendium of secret oracles that he adapted to the circumstances. But he was also a political adviser and even an envoy; Aristotle tells us that some people associated him with Lycurgus, Charondas, and Zaleucus as one of the first experts on legislative questions.

Thus we cannot imagine the beginnings of law apart from a certain religious climate: the mystical movement arose in response to a more stringent communal conscience. It expressed a new group sensibility with respect to murder, an anguish before the acts of violence and hatred bred by private revenge, a sense of being collectively involved, collectively threatened each time blood was shed, a determination to regulate relations between *gene* and to break down their self-interest. This mystical ferment, however, could continue only in the very narrowly circumscribed environment of the cults. It did not give rise to a widespread movement of religious renewal that ultimately embraced politics. What happened was the reverse. Aspirations toward communal solidarity reached more directly into the social sphere, in a legislative and reform effort. But in thus remodeling public life, those aspirations themselves were transformed and secularized. In becoming embodied in judicial and political institutions, they lent themselves to the work of conceptual elaboration and were shifted to the level of pragmatic thought.

Louis Gernet has ably shown the particular intellectual changes brought about by the advent of law as we now know it.[9] In the legal proceedings of the Archaic period, the *gene* confronted one another not with arms but with ritual formulas and traditional evidence— oaths, co-swearing, bearing of witness. Such evidence was decisive; it had religious force, automatically ensuring success in any contest if it were properly used. The judge was merely a referee; he was restricted to verifying and proclaiming the victor in a test of strength. He did not inquire into the background of the quarrel, reconstruct the matter in dispute, or acquaint himself with the facts. But with the rise of the city, the judge came to represent the body of citizens, the community as a whole. Then, as the personification of that impersonal entity superior to parties, he could decide a case according to his conscience and the law, and the very notions of evidence, testimony, and judgment were radically transformed. The judge had to bring the true facts into the open and then base his verdict on them. He no longer asked witnesses to be co-swearers, declaring joint responsibility with one of the two parties, but to report the facts. With this totally new conception of evidence and testimony, legal proceedings brought into operation a whole technique of proof, of reconstruction of the plausible and the probable, of deduction from clues or indications—and judicial activity contributed to the development of the notion of objective truth, with which the old "protolegal" proceedings had been unacquainted.

[9]Gernet, *Droit et société*, pp. 61–81.

CHAPTER SIX

The Structure of
the Human Cosmos

Religious ferment not only contributed to the birth of law, but also provided the impetus for a consideration of moral and political questions. The dread of defilement (whose role in the origin of laws concerning homicide has been noted) was expressed most intensely in the mystical yearning for a life free of all fleshly contact. In the same way, the popular ideal of austerity that emerged in reaction to the growth of commerce, the display of luxuries, and the high-handedness of the rich is seen in extreme form in the asceticism extolled in some religious organizations. The cult circles thus helped to shape a new image of *arete* [virtue]. Aristocratic virtue was a natural quality associated with high birth, and was manifested in courage in battle and an opulent way of life. In the religious groups, *arete* not only shed its traditional warlike aspect, but was now defined by its opposition to everything rep-

In this chapter I have made extensive use of information provided by L. Gernet in an unpublished series of lectures on the origins of political thought among the Greeks, given at the Ecole Pratique des Hautes Etudes in 1951.

resented by the ideal of *habrosyne* [refinement], such as sensitive behavior and manners. Virtue was now regarded as the fruit of a long and arduous *askesis* [training], of a hard, strict discipline, or *melete*. It set in motion an *epimeleia*, a vigilant self-control, an unflagging readiness to flee the temptations of pleasure, *hedone*, the lure of indolence and sensuality, *malakia* and *tryphe*, and to choose a life wholly dedicated to *ponos*, arduous effort.

These are the same rigorous tendencies that we see in a somewhat exaggerated form among the cults, where they appeared as a discipline of *askesis* that enabled the initiate to escape the injustices of this life, to break free of the cycle of reincarnation and return to the divine source of things. We recognize them at work in ordinary life, minus any eschatological concerns, tempering behavior, values, and institutions. Pomp, ease, and pleasure were rejected; luxury in dress, in one's dwelling, in food and drink were forbidden. How furiously wealth was denounced! But the target of the denunciation was the social consequences of wealth—the evils it bred within the group, the divisions and hatreds it stirred up in the city, the condition of *stasis* [civil discord] it brought about a sort of natural law. Wealth had replaced all the aristocratic values: marriage, honors, privileges, reputation, power—wealth could win them all. Now it was money that mattered, money that made the man. But unlike all other "powers," wealth admitted of no limit: nothing in it could set a bound, restrict it, or make it complete. The essence of wealth was excess, which was also the shape taken by *hybris* in the world. This was the obsessively recurring theme in the moral thought of the sixth century. The words of Solon, which had become proverbs ("No end to wealth; *koros,* surfeit, begets *hybris*"), were echoed by Theognis ("Those who today have the most want to have twice as much; wealth, *ta chremata,* turns a man to madness, *aphrosyne*"). He who has, desires yet more. Ultimately wealth has no object but itself. Created to satisfy the needs of life, as a mere means of subsistence, it becomes its own end, a universal, insatiable, boundless craving that nothing will ever be able to assuage. At the root of wealth one therefore discovers a corrupted disposition, a perverse will, a *pleonexia*—the desire to have more than others, more than one's share, to have everything. In Greek eyes, *ploutos* [wealth] was bound up with a kind of disaster—not an economic disaster, but the necessary consequence of a character trait, an *ethos,* the logic of a certain kind of behavior. *Koros, hybris, pleonexia* were the irrational forms assumed by aristocratic arrogance in the Iron Age—that spirit of *eris* [strife] which now bred not high-minded emulation, but only injustice, oppression, *dysnomia* [disorder].

The idea of *sophrosyne* took shape in contrast to the *hybris* of the rich. It consisted of moderation, proportion, fair limits, the golden mean. "Nothing in excess" was the motto of the new wisdom. This valuing of the moderate, the mean, gave the Greek idea of *arete* almost a "bourgeois" aspect: it was the middle class that was able to play a moderating role in the city by striking a balance between extremes on both sides—the minority of the rich who wanted to hold onto everything, the mass of people who had nothing and who wanted to get everything. Those called *hoi mesoi* were not only the members of a particular social class, midway between destitution and affluence: they represented a human type and embodied new civic values, as the rich embodied the extravagance of *hybris*. From their median position in the group, the *mesoi* had the role of establishing a balance, a connecting link between the two parties that were tearing the city apart because each claimed all *arche* for itself. Solon, himself a man of the "center," set out to be arbiter, mediator, and reconciler. If he succeeded in apportioning *arche* among the various factions according to their respective merits, he would then have brought the harmony of the cosmos to a *polis* set upon by *dysnomia*. But this balanced distribution, this *eunomia*, imposed limits on the ambitions of those moved by the spirit of excess; it drew a line beyond which they might not step. At the center of the state stood Solon like an immovable pillar, a *horos* [boundary stone] marking the line between two opposing mobs, which neither could cross. Corresponding to *sophrosyne*, the virtue of the happy medium, is the image of a political order that sets up an equilibrium between opposing forces, establishing an accord between rival groups. But like the legal process, the new form of arbitration presupposed a judge who, in handing down his decision and if necessary enforcing it, referred to a law superior to the parties, a *dike* that was necessarily the same for everyone. "I wrote," Solon said, "the same laws for the *kakos* [low] and the *agathos* [high], setting down impartial justice for each." To preserve the rule of a law that was common to all, Solon refused the office of tyrant, which was well within his reach. How was he to take into his own hands, the hands of one man, the *arche* that must remain *en meso*? What Solon accomplished, he did in the name of the community, by the force of law, *kratei nomou*,

joining together might with right, *bian kai diken*. Kratos
and Bia, the two ancient attendants of Zeus—who might
not leave their places beside his throne for even an in-
stant, since they embodied all that was absolute, irresist-
ible, and irrational in the sovereign's power—had passed
into the service of the law. Now they were servants of
nomos, which reigned in place of the king at the center of
the city. Because of its relation to *dike*, *nomos* still had a
certain religious connotation; but it was expressed also
and above all in a practical effort to legislate, a rational
attempt to bring an end to conflict, to balance antagonis-
tic social forces, to reconcile opposing human attitudes.
Evidence of this political "rationalism" is to be found in
Solon's fourth fragment.[1] We have come a long way from
Hesiod's good king, whose religious virtue alone could
resolve all quarrels and summon forth peace and all of
earth's blessings. Justice had seemed then to be entirely
natural and self-regulating. It was human wickedness,
the spirit of *hybris*, the insatiable thirst for wealth that
naturally brought forth disorder, by a process whose
every phase could be marked out in advance: thus injustice gave rise to the enslavement of the masses, which in
turn gave rise to rebellion. To reestablish order and
hesychia [tranquillity], moderation must thus simultaneously crush the arrogance of the rich and put an end to
the enslavement of the *demos*, yet without yielding to sub-
version. Such was the teaching that Solon set before the
eyes of all citizens. The lesson might be temporarily mis-
understood or rejected, but the sage had faith in the
power of time: once the truth had been made public—or,

[1]See G. Vlastos, "Solonian Justice," *Classical Philology*, 41 (1946),
65–83.

as he put it, had been laid down *es to meson*—the day would come when the Athenians would acknowledge it.

With Solon, Dike and Sophrosyne came down from heaven to take up residence in the agora. That is to say, they would henceforth be accountable. The Greeks would most certainly continue to invoke them; but they would never again refrain from subjecting them to discussion.

Through this marked secularization of moral thought, the idea of a virtue such as *sophrosyne* could be renewed and clarified. In Homer, *sophrosyne* had the very general meaning of good sense: the gods restored it to one who had lost it, just as they could cause the shrewdest minds to lose it. [2] But before being reinterpreted by the sages in a political context, the idea seems to have been elaborated in certain religious circles. There it designated a return to a state of calm, stability, and self-control after a period of upheaval and demonic possession. The means employed were the kind we have noted: music, song, dancing, purification rites. Sometimes more direct means could be used to produce a shock effect. In the shrine of Heracles at Thebes, Pausanias saw a stone that Athena was said to have thrown at the head of the raging hero when, driven wild by *mania,* he slaughtered his own children and was about to kill Amphitryon. [3] This stone, which numbed and calmed him, was called *sophronister.* Orestes' recovery took place in somewhat different circumstances. During his madness after murdering his mother, the unfortunate hero came to a place named for the Furies: *Maniai.* There he stopped and cut off one of his fingers (which in

[2] *Odyssey*, XXIII, 13.
[3] Pausanias, IX, 11, 2.

Pausanias' time was still represented by a stone set on a mound called *mnema dactylou*, the tomb of the finger). In that place, known as Ake, the Cure, he regained *sophrosyne*. Pausanias adds the following detail: as long as the Furies had Orestes in their possession and rendered him *ekphron*, out of his mind, they appeared black to him; once he had cut off his finger and become *sophron*, sound in mind, he saw them as white.[4] This same interplay between defilement and purification, possession and recovery, madness and sound mind, is evident even in the setting of the cave where the soothsayer Melampous, by secret rituals and *katharmoi* [purifications], calmed the frenzy of Proitos' daughters: on one side flowed the waters of the Styx, the river of defilement, bringing disease and death to every living creature, and on the other the spring Alyssos, whose beneficent waters cured the insane and all those possessed by the frenzy of *lyssa*.[5] But in thus being defined in contrast to a madness that was also pollution, *sophrosyne*'s moderation took on an ascetic quality in the religious climate of the cults. As the virtue of constraint and abstinence, it consisted of turning aside from evil, avoiding all defilement: not only refusing the criminal temptations that an evil spirit can arouse in us, but abstaining from sexual intercourse, reining in the promptings of *eros* and all the appetites of the flesh, and serving an apprenticeship in self-control, the conquest of self, by undergoing ordeals of initiation into the Way of Life. The self-mastery of which *sophrosyne* is composed seemed to imply, if not a dualism, at least a certain ten-

---

[4]Pausanias, VIII, 34, 1ff.
[5]Pausanias, VIII, 17, 6ff., and 19, 2-3.

sion between two opposing elements in human nature: those pertaining to *thymos*, the affections, emotions, and passions (favorite themes of lyric poetry), and those associated with a considered discretion, a reasoned calculation (as extolled by the gnomic poets). These powers of the soul were not on the same plane. *Thymos* was formed for obedience and submission. The cure and prevention of madness involved methods of "persuading" *thymos*, of making it amenable to discipline and receptive to command, so that it would never again be tempted to rebel, or to assert a supremacy that would bring the soul to disorder. These techniques constituted a *paideia* [education] that was not limited to individuals. To them it brought health and stability; it made the soul "continent," keeping in subjection the part intended to obey. But by the same token it took on a social aspect, a political function, since the evils from which the community suffered were the incontinence of the rich and the subversive spirit of the "spiteful." By doing away with both, *sophrosyne* produced a peaceful and harmonious city, in which the rich, far from always desiring more, gave away their surplus to the poor, and the masses, instead of rebelling, agreed to submit to their betters, who had the right to possess more. This preoccupation with political questions could not have been alien to the principles of certain cults. Among the Olympian and Eleusinian divinities in the sanctuary of Demeter at Pergamum, where the religious fraternity that conducted the worship was required to sing Orphic hymns (as the Lycomids had to do at Athens), were a number of Orphic gods who personified abstract ideas. Among them were two pairs, Arete [Virtue] and Sophrosyne, Pistis [Trust] and

89

Homonoia.[6] This grouping is worth emphasizing. In the work of Theognis, Pistis is also associated with Sophrosyne.[7] This idea is the subjective aspect of *homonoia*, and as such is social and political: the trust that citizens have for one another is the inner, psychological counterpart of social harmony. In the soul as in the city, it is through the power of Pistis that the lower elements are persuaded to obey those who have the function of command, and willingly subject themselves to a rule that keeps them in their subordinate position.

In general, however, it was outside the cults that *sophrosyne* acquired its precise moral and political significance. A cleavage opened up very early between two sharply divergent currents of thought. One was concerned with individual salvation, the other with that of the city. On the one hand were the religious groups on the fringes of the community, turning in upon themselves in their search for purity; on the other were the circles directly involved in public life, who had to deal with the divisions within the state, and who used such traditional ideas as *sophrosyne* in a way that gave them a new political content and a form that was practical rather than religious.

In an institution such as the Spartan *agoge* [educational system], *sophrosyne* already showed an essentially social character. It entailed behavior that was regulated, con-

---

[6]See W. K. C. Guthrie, *Orpheus and Greek Religion: A Study of the Orphic Movement*, 2d ed., revised (London, 1952), pp. 259ff.; H. Usener, *Götternamen: Versuch einer Lehre von der Religiösen Begriffsbildung* (Bonn, 1896), p. 368.

[7]Theognis, 1137–1138.

trolled, and marked by the reserve a young man was expected to maintain in all circumstances: in his walk, in his glance, in his talk, in his behavior toward women and his elders, in the agora, in regard to pleasures and to drinking. Xenophon evokes just such solemn reserve when he compares the Lacedaemonian *kouros*, walking in silence with eyes lowered, to a statue of a virgin. The dignity of one's behavior had an institutional significance; it externalized a moral attitude and a psychological mold that were felt as obligations: the future citizen must be trained to rule his passions, his emotions, and his instincts. The Lacedaemonian *agoge* was specifically designed to test this self-mastery. *Sophrosyne* thus held up each individual to a common model in his relations with others, consistent with the city's image of "political man." The citizen's reserved behavior was as far removed from the easygoingness and ludicrous vulgarity of the common herd as it was from the aristocrat's haughty arrogance. The new style in human relations conformed to the standards of discipline, balance, and moderation expressed by such aphorisms as "Know thyself," "Nothing in excess," and "Moderation is best." The sages' role was to identify and put into words, in poetry or maxims, the values that remained more or less implicit in the citizen's conduct and social life. But their intellectual efforts not only led to a conceptual formulation; they put the moral problem into a political context and linked it with the development of public life. They were caught up in civil strife and anxious to bring it to an end by their work as legislators. It was thus as a consequence of a social situation, in the framework of a history marked by a conflict of forces, by a confrontation of groups, that the sages worked out their ethical beliefs and arrived at a pragmatic definition of the conditions under which order might be established in the city.

To understand the social realities that overlay the ideal of *sophrosyne*, and how the notions of *metrion* [the mean], *pistis* [trust], *homonoia* [unanimity], and *eunomia* [law and order] were blended to form a whole, it is necessary to consider such constitutional reforms as those of Solon. They made a place for the equality—*isotes*—that had already appeared as one of the foundations of the new conception of order. Without *isotes* there would be no city because there would be no *philia* [friendship]. "The man who is an equal," wrote Solon, "is incapable of starting a war." But this was a hierarchical equality—or, as the Greeks would say, an equality that was geometrical rather than arithmetical. The essential idea was actually "proportion." The city formed an organized whole, a cosmos, which was harmonious if each of its constituent parts was in its place and had the share of power it was due by virtue of its own quality. "To the *demos*," Solon said, "I gave as much *kratos* [power] (or *geras* [privilege]) as it needs, without diminishing or adding to its *time* [prestige]." Thus there was no equal right either to municipal offices (the highest being reserved for the best) or to landed property: Solon rejected a distribution of land that would have "given the *kakoi* [the lowborn] and the *esthloi* [the highborn] equal shares of the richest lands." Where, then, was equality? It lay in the fact that the law, now set down, was the same for all citizens, and that all could take part in the courts of justice and the assembly. Heretofore it had been "pride," the "unruly spirit" of the rich, that governed social relations. Solon was the first to refuse to obey it or let himself be "persuaded" by it. Now it was *dike* that determined the reapportionment of *timai* [honors and offices]; written laws replaced the test of strength in which the powerful always won, and established their own standard of impartiality, their requirement of fairness. *Homonoia* or concord was a harmony brought about by proportions that Solon made all the more precise by giving them a quasi-numerical form: the four classes into which the citizens were divided, and which corresponded to grades of honor, were based on the measures used for agricultural products: five hundred measures for the highest class, three hundred for the *hippeis*, two hundred for the *zeugitai*. The accord of the city's various factions was possible because the intermediate group—the middle classes—did not want to see either the higher or the lower class seize control of *arche*. The lawgiver and the law he promulgated were themselves the expression of this will of the middle, this "proportional mean" that gave the city its center of gravity.

The development of moral and political thought followed the same lines: for relations based on strength people tried to substitute connections of a "rational" kind, by establishing in every sphere a system of regulation based on moderation and aimed toward accommodating and "equalizing" the various kinds of exchange that made up the fabric of social life.

A remark attributed to Solon sheds light on the significance of this change, which had been effected, as

Plutarch notes, by reason and law: *hypo logou kai nomou metabole.*[8] Anacharsis had mocked the Athenian sage who imagined that written laws could curb the *adikia* [injustice] and *pleonexia* [greed] of his fellow citizens: like cobwebs, the laws would restrain the weak and small, while the rich and powerful would tear them apart. Solon countered with the example of conditions with which two contracting parties complied because neither had anything to gain by violating them.[9] So the city's task was to promulgate rules that codified the relations between individuals according to the same practical principles of reciprocal advantage that governed the drawing up of a contract.

As E. Will has shown, it is within the framework of this general process of codification and proportion that we must place the origin of money in the true sense of the word—that is, a state currency, issued and guaranteed by the city.[10] The economic consequences of this event are well known: on the economic level it operated as an agent of radical change, orienting Greek society in the direction of mercantilism. But at the beginning, given its social, moral, and intellectual significance, the establishment of a currency was an integral part of the "legislators'" general undertaking. The aris-

---

[8]Plutarch, "The Life of Solon," XIV, 5.

[9]Plutarch, "The Life of Solon," V, 4-5.

[10]E. Will, *Korinthiaka: Recherches sur l'histoire et la civilisation de Corinthe des origines aux guerres médiques* (Paris, 1955), pp. 495–502; "De l'aspect éthique de l'origine grecque de la monnaie," *Revue historique,* 212 (1954), 209ff.; "Réflexions et hypothèses sur les origines du monnayage," *Revue numismatique,* 17 (1955), 5–23.

tocratic privilege of issuing stamped bullion was appropriated for the benefit of the community as the state seized the sources of precious metal and substituted the city's seal for the devices of the nobles. At the same time it was a means of codifying, regulating, and coordinating the exchange of goods and services among citizens according to an exact numerical valuation; perhaps it was also, as Will suggests, an attempt to equalize wealth to some extent by putting specie into circulation, or by altering its value without resort to unlawful confiscation. On the intellectual level, for the old image of wealth as *hybris*—so charged with affective force and religious implications—legal tender substituted the abstract idea of *nomisma*, a social standard of value, a rational contrivance that allowed for a common measure of diverse realities, and thus equalized exchange as a social relationship.

It is quite remarkable that in their polemics the two great opposing currents in the Greek world—the one aristocratic in inspiration, the other democratic in spirit—both took their stand on the same ground and made the same appeal to equity, *isotes*. The aristocratic tendency was to envisage the city, in the perspective of a Solonian *eunomia*, as a cosmos made up of sundry parts, maintained in hierarchical order by the law. *Homonoia* was analogous to a harmonic chord, based on a musical sort of relationship: 2/1, 3/2, 4/3. Moderation would harmonize forces that were by nature unequal by ensuring that the stronger did not go to excess. The harmony of *eunomia* thus implied the recognition of a certain dualism in the social body as in the individual, a polarity between good and evil, and the need to ensure the predominance of the better over the worse. This was the orientation that triumphed in Pythagoreanism;[11] it also governed the theory of *sophrosyne* as Plato set it forth in the *Republic*.[12] *Sophrosyne* was not a quality peculiar to any one party within the state, but the harmony of the whole, which made the city a cosmos and gave it self-mastery, in the same way that an individual was said to be master of his own desires and diversions. Comparing it to singing in harmony, Plato defined it as "an agreement between the naturally superior and inferior voices as to which should lead, both in the state and in the individual." A text by Archytas, the Pythagorean statesman, brings us down from the philosophical heights of the *Republic* and a little closer to social reality. He shows how the practice of commercial exchange and its necessary regulation by contract contributed to the idea of a measurement of social relations, a precise evaluation of the relations among the activities, functions, services, benefits, and honors of the various social orders, according to the principles of proportional equality. "Once discovered," wrote Archytas, "rational computation [*logismos*] puts an end to the condition of *stasis* and introduces *homonoia*; for there is truly no more *pleonexia*, and *isotes* is achieved; and it is equality that permits business to be carried on in matters of contractual exchange. Thanks to all this, the poor receive from the mighty and the rich give to those in need, all groups having the *pistis* that by these means they will have *isotes*, equality."

[11]See A. Delatte, *Essai sur la politique pythagoricienne* (Liège and Paris, 1922).

[12]Plato, *Republic*, IV, 430d ff.

Here, indeed, we see how social intercourse, now likened to a contractual bond rather than a law of dominance and submission, was expressed in terms of reciprocity, of reversibility. According to Aristotle's account of the situation at Tarentum, Archytas' intent was in practice to keep individual possession of property in the hands of the "best," so long as they permitted its use by the mass of the poor; in such an arrangement, everyone got something. For believers in *eunomia*, equity was introduced into social relations as a result of a moral and psychological transformation of the elite: instead of seeking power and wealth, the "best" were molded by a philosophical *paideia* not to wish to have more (*pleonektein*), but on the contrary to give with open-handed generosity to the poor, for whom *pleonektein* was literally impossible.[13] In this way the lower classes were kept in their proper subordinate position, but without being subjected to any injustice. The equality thus achieved remained proportional to merit.

The democratic current went further when it defined all citizens, without regard to fortune or quality, as "equals" having precisely the same rights to take part in all aspects of public life. Such is the ideal of *isonomia*, which envisaged equality in terms of the simplest relationship: 1/1. The only "correct measure" capable of harmonizing relations among citizens was full and complete equality. The problem was no longer, as it had been earlier, to find a scale for apportioning power by merit, one that produced a harmonic concord between different and even discordant elements, but strictly to equalize

---

[13]Aristotle, *Politics*, II, 1267b.

participation in *arche* and access to public offices for all citizens, to eliminate all the differences that had set the various parts of the city against one another, and to blend and merge them so that on the political level citizens were no longer differentiated in any respect. This was the objective achieved by Cleisthenes' reforms; they set up a comprehensive political structure that in its neatness and coherence, its utter practicality, promised to be the solution to the problem of devising a law that would regulate the city so that it would be one in the multiplicity of its citizens and they would be equal in their unavoidable diversity.

Throughout the period that preceded Cleisthenes, from the archonship of Solon to the tyranny and then the fall of the Pisistratids, Athenian history had been dominated by a conflict among three factions, each ranged against the others in their struggle for power. What did these factions represent? They were the expression of a complex set of social realities that are not accurately covered by our own political and economic categories. They denoted, first of all, tribal and territorial affiliations. Each of the three factions took its name from one of the three regions into which Attica was divided. The *pediakoi* were the plainsmen, the people of the *pedion*—actually the inhabitants of the city and of the fertile lands surrounding it; the *paralioi* lived along the coast; and the *diakrioi* were highlanders, people of the hinterland—that is, the outlying demes farthest from the urban center. Corresponding to these territorial divisions were differences in way of life, social customs, and political orientation: the *pediakoi* were aristocrats, defending their privileges as *eupatridai* and their interests as landholders; the *paralioi* made up the new social stratum of the *mesoi,* who sought to avoid the triumph of either extreme; and the *diacrioi* made up the party of the common people, bringing together the population of *thetes*—small farmers, woodcutters, and charcoal burners—many of whom had no place in the tribal structure and were not yet assimilated into the framework of the aristocratic city. The three factions arose as clients of the great aristocratic families they served and whose rivalry dominated the political scene.

Among these factions, which amounted to distinct and opposing "parties" within the state, open conflict alternated with accommodation until Cleisthenes reconstituted the *polis* on a new basis.[14] The old tribal structure was abolished. In place of the four Ionian tribes that made up Attic society, Cleisthenes set up a system of ten tribes. As before, each tribe consisted of three *trittyes* [voting districts], but now all the demes of Attica were divided among these districts. The city was thus no longer organized according to connections between *gene* and blood ties. Tribes and demes were established on a purely geographical basis; they brought together dwellers on the same soil rather than blood relatives, as in the *gene* and the phratries, which continued to exist in their old form but now were outside the strictly political

[14]One compromise solution seems to have been to assign the archonship to the leaders of the three rival clans in turn; on this point, see Benjamin D. Meritt, "Greek Inscription: An Early Archon List," *Hesperia,* 8 (1939), 59–65; H. T. Wade Gery, "Miltiades," *Journal of Hellenic Studies,* 71 (1951), 212–221. This attempt at a balanced division of power among opposing factions may be compared with one Aristotle reports from an earlier period: the nomination of ten archons—five *eupatridai* [nobles], three *agroikoi* [farmers], and two *demiurgoi* [artisans] (*The Athenian Constitution,* XIII, 2).

structure. And each of the ten newly formed tribes was an amalgamation of the three different "parties" into which the city had previously been divided. So of the three *trittyes* of which a tribe was composed, the first of necessity came from the coastal region, the second from the hinterland, the third from the urban area and its environs. In this way each tribe embodied a cross section of the populations, regional characteristics, and kinds of activity that made up the city. As Aristotle noted, if Cleisthenes had set up twelve tribes instead of ten, he would then have assigned the citizens to the *trittyes* already in existence (the four old tribes had in fact consisted of twelve *trittyes*), and thus would not have succeeded in unifying the body of citizens by mixing them together: *anamisgesthai to plethos.*[15]

The administrative structure, then, was a response to a deliberate intent to merge and unify the social body. Moreover, an arbitrary division of civic time allowed the complete equalization of *arche* among all the groups thus established. The lunar calendar continued to regulate religious life. But the administrative year was divided into ten periods of either thirty-six or thirty-seven days, each corresponding to one of the ten tribes. The membership in the Council of Four Hundred was raised to five hundred, fifty for each tribe, so that during the ten periods of the year each of the tribes in turn made up the standing committee of the council. With Cleisthenes, the egalitarian ideal was directly linked to political reality at the same time that it was expressed in the abstract concept of *isonomia*; it inspired a reshaping of

[15]Aristotle, *The Athenian Constitution*, XXI, 3.

institutions. The world of social relations thus formed a coherent system, governed by numerical relations and correspondences that permitted the citizens to declare themselves "the same," to enter into relations of mutual equality, symmetry, and reciprocity, and together to form a unified cosmos. The *polis* was seen as a homogeneous whole, without hierarchy, without rank, without differentiation. *Arche* was no longer concentrated in a single figure at the apex of the social structure, but was distributed equally throughout the entire realm of public life, in that common space where the city had its center, its *meson*. Sovereignty passed from one group to another, from one individual to another, in a regular cycle, so that command and obedience, rather than being opposed to each other as two absolutes, became the two inseparable aspects of one reversible relationship. Under the law of *isonomia*, the social realm had the form of a centered and circular cosmos, in which each citizen, because he was like all the others, would have to cover the entire circuit as time went round, successively occupying and surrendering each of the symmetrical positions that made up civic space.

CHAPTER SEVEN

Cosmogonies and Myths of Sovereignty

In the history of humankind, beginnings ordinarily elude us. But if the advent of philosophy in Greece marked the decline of mythological thought and the beginning of rational understanding, we can fix the date and place of birth of Greek reason—establish its civil status. It was at the beginning of the sixth century, in Ionian Miletus, that such men as Thales, Anaximander, and Anaximenes ushered in a new way of thinking about nature. They made it the object of a detached and systematic investigation (a *historia*) and offered a comprehensive view of it (a *theoria*). The explanations they proposed for the origin of the world, its composition and structure, and all meteorological phenomena were unencumbered by the dramatic machinery of earlier theogonies and cosmogonies. The figures of the great primordial powers were now obliterated. Gone were the supernatural agents whose adventures, struggles, and exploits formed the web of creation myths that traced the emergence of the world and the establishment of order; gone even any allusion to the gods that were linked to the forces of nature by the beliefs and observances of the official religion. For the "natural philosophers" of Ionia, a spirit of positivism pervaded the whole of existence from the outset. Nothing existed that was not nature, *physis*. The human, the divine, and the natural worlds made up a unified, homogeneous universe, all on the same plane; they were the parts or aspects of one and the same *physis*, which everywhere brought into play the same powers and revealed the same vital force. The ways in which *physis* had come into being and been diversified and ordered were entirely accessible to human intelligence: nature had not functioned "in the beginning" otherwise than it still functioned every day, when fire dried a wet garment or when a sieve was shaken and the larger particles were separated from the rest. As there was but one *physis*, which excluded the very notion of anything supernatural, so there was but a single temporality. The ancient and the primordial were stripped of their grandeur and mystery; they had the reassuring banality of familiar phenomena. To mythological thought, daily experience was illumined and given meaning by exemplary deeds performed by the gods "in the beginning." For the Ionians, the comparison was reversed. The primal events, the forces that produced the cosmos, were conceived in the image of the facts that could be observed today, and could be explained in the same way. It was no longer the beginning that illumined and transfigured the everyday; it was the everyday that made the beginning intelligible, by supplying models for an understanding of how the world had been shaped and set in order.

This intellectual revolution appears to have been so sudden and so radical that it has been considered inexplicable in terms of historical causality: we speak of a Greek miracle. All of a sudden, on the soil of Ionia, *logos* presumably broke free of myth, as the scales fell from the blind man's eyes. And the light of that reason, revealed once and for all, has never ceased to guide the progress of the human mind. "The early Ionian teachers," writes Burnet, " . . . first pointed the way which Europe has followed ever since."[1] And he says elsewhere, "It would be completely false to seek the origins of Ionian science in some mythic conception."

This interpretation is challenged point by point by F. M. Cornford. According to Cornford, the earliest philosophy remains closer to mythological construct than to scientific theory. Ionian natural philosophy had nothing in common, in either inspiration or methods, with what we call science; specifically, it knew nothing whatever of experimentation. Nor was it the product of reason's naive and spontaneous reflection on nature. It transposed into secular form, with a more abstract vocabulary, the concept of the world worked out by religion. The cosmologies simply took up and extended the main themes of the creation myths. They provided an answer to the same kind of question; they did not inquire, as science does, into the laws of nature; like myth, they wondered how order had been established, how it had been possible for the cosmos to emerge from chaos. From the creation myths the Milesians took not only an image of the universe but a whole conceptual apparatus and explanatory schemata: behind the "elements" of *physis* loom the old gods of mythology. In becoming nature, the

[1]John Burnet, *Early Greek Philosophy*, 3d ed. (London, 1920), p.v.

elements shed the trappings of individualized deities, but they were still active, animate powers, and were still deeply felt to be divine; when *physis* was at work, it was imbued with the wisdom and justice that were the attributes of Zeus. The Homeric world was set in order by the apportioning of realms and functions among the chief gods: to Zeus the dazzling light of the sky (*aither*), to Hades the hazy shadows (*aer*), to Poseidon the watery element, and to all three jointly Gaia, the earth, where humans live along with the other mortal creatures. The Ionian cosmos was divided into regions and seasons among elemental powers that were variously opposed, counterbalanced, or commingled. This is no vague analogy. Cornford's analysis reveals close correspondences between the *Theogony* of Hesiod and the philosophy of Anaximander. True, one still spoke of divine generations while the other described natural processes, refusing to play on the ambiguity of such terms as *phyein* and *genesis*, which mean "to bear" as well as "to produce"—birth as well as origin. As long as these various meanings were still mingled, it was possible to speak of becoming in terms of sexual union, and to explain a phenomenon by designating a father and mother and drawing up a family tree. Nonetheless, however important this difference between the natural philosopher and the theologian may be, the general structure of their thought remained the same. Both posited at the beginning an inchoate state in which nothing had yet made its appearance (the Chaos of Hesiod; Nyx, Erebos, or Tartaros, in the theogonies attributed to Orpheus, Musaeus, and Epimenides; Apeiron, the Undefined, of Anaximander). From this primordial unity, by progressive segregation and differentiation, paired opposites emerged—dark and light, hot and cold, dry and wet, dense and rarefied, high and low . . . —which would delineate various categories and regions of the world: the sky (warm and bright), the air (dark and cold), the earth (dry), the ocean (watery). These opposites, which had come into being through a process of separation, could also unite and mingle to produce certain phenomena, such as the birth and death of every living thing—vegetable, animal, or human.

But it was not only the schema of the whole that was essentially preserved. Even in the details, the symmetrical development and correspondence of certain themes show the persistence in the philosopher's thought of mythic representations that had lost none of their evocative force. [2] Sexual generation, the cosmic egg, the tree of life, the separation of a previously mingled earth and sky—all were implicit images that are visible like a watermark behind the "physical" explanations given by an Anaximander for the formation of the world: a seed or germ (*gonimon*) that was capable of generating heat and cold had been secreted (*apokrinesthai*) from the Apeiron. At the center of the germ was the cold, in the form of *aer;* on the outside, encircling the cold, heat developed (*periphyenai*) as a shell of fire similar to the bark (*phloios*) that encases a tree. A time came when this fiery spherical casing separated (*aporregnysthai*) from the nucleus within, and, like a broken shell, splintered into rings of fire, which are the stars. Scholars have noted the use of embryological terms that simultaneously evoke and

[2]See Marcel de Corte, "Mythe et philosophie chez Anaximandre," *Laval théologique et philosophique*, 14 (1958 [1960]), 9–29.

rationalize the themes of sexual generation and sacred marriage: *gonimon, apokrinesthai, aporregnysthai,* and *phloios.* The last term is derived from *phleo,* a verb connected with the idea of generation, and may refer to the embryonic sac, the shell of an egg, the bark of a tree, and in general to any skin that encloses a plant or animal organism like a membrane as it grows.[3]

Despite these echoes and analogies, however, there is no real continuity between myth and philosophy. The philosopher was not satisfied to repeat in terms of *physis* what the theologian had expressed in terms of divine power. Corresponding to the change in tone and the use of a secular vocabulary was a new mental attitude, a different intellectual climate. With the Milesians, the origin and ordering of the world for the first time took the form of an explicitly posed problem to which an answer must be supplied without mystery, an answer gauged to human intelligence, capable of being aired and publicly debated before the mass of citizens like any question of everyday life. They thus posited a function of understanding free of any concern with ritual. The "natural philosophers" deliberately ignored the domain of religion. Their quest no longer had anything to do with those religious practices to which myth, despite its relative autonomy, always remained bound to some degree.

The desacralization of knowledge, the advent of a kind of thought foreign to religion—these were not isolated and incomprehensible phenomena. In its form, philosophy is directly linked to the spiritual realm that we

[3]H. G. Baldry, "Embryological Analogies in Presocratic Cosmogony," *Classical Quarterly,* 26 (1932), 27–34.

have seen give order to the city, and which was so distinctly characterized by the secularization and rationalization of social life. But philosophy's dependence on the institutions of the *polis* is no less marked in its content. If it is true that the Milesians borrowed from mythology, they also profoundly altered the image of the universe by integrating it within a spatial framework, according to a more geometrical model. In constructing the new cosmologies, they made use of ideas elaborated by moral and political thought, projecting onto the world of nature that conception of order and law whose success in the city had made the human world a cosmos.

The Greek theogonies and cosmogonies, like the cosmologies that came after them, accorded with creation tales that told of the progressive emergence of an orderly world. But also, and above all, they were myths of sovereignty. They exalted the power of a god who ruled over all the universe; they told of his birth, his struggles, his victory. In every domain, whether natural, social, or ritual, order was the product of that victory of the sovereign divinity. If the world was no longer given over to instability and confusion, it was because the god no longer had to fight battles against monsters and rivals; his supremacy was now so manifestly assured that no one could ever again question it. Hesiod's *Theogony* thus reads like a hymn to the glory of Zeus the king. The defeat of the Titans and of Typhon, alike vanquished by the son of Kronos, not only serves to complete the structure of the poem and bring it to a conclusion; each episode also recapitulates and summarizes the architecture of the cosmogonic myth. Each victory of Zeus is a creation of the world. The tale of the battle that pits the two rival generations of Titans and Olympians against each other explicitly evokes the return of the universe to an original state of inchoate disorder. Unsettled by combat, the primordial powers, Gaia, Ouranos, Pontos, Okeanos, and Tartaros, who previously were differentiated and assigned their own places, are again flung together. Gaia and Ouranos, whose separation is described by Hesiod, seem to be rejoined with one another and made one again as though they had fallen apart. It might be supposed that the underworld had erupted into daylight: that the visible universe, instead of being a stable, orderly scene spread out between the two fixed strata that bound it—the earth beneath, the abode of mortals, and the heavens above, the seat of the gods—had resumed its earlier look of chaos: a dark, vertiginous abyss, a bottomless hole, a chasm of directionless space where the whirlwinds blow everywhere at once and at random.[4] Zeus's victory puts everything back in place. The infernal Titans are dispatched in chains to the windswept pit of Tartaros. The gusts can now toss about in endless disorder in the underground abyss in which earth, sky, and sea thrust down their common roots. Poseidon has locked up the Titans behind the doors that seal off forever the dwelling places of night. Chaos will never again threaten to rise into the light to overwhelm the visible world.

The battle against Typhon (this is an interpolation that probably dates from the end of the seventh century) takes up comparable themes. In a suggestive discussion,

[4]Hesiod, *Theogony*, 700–740.

Cornford has compared this episode to the battle of Marduk against Tiamat. Like Tiamat, Typhon represents the powers of confusion and disorder, the return to formlessness and chaos. It is easy to imagine what would have befallen the world if this monster of a thousand voices, the son of Ge and Tartaros, had managed to rule over gods and men in place of Zeus: from his remains are born the winds that, rather than blowing steadily and regularly in the same direction (as Notus, Boreas, and Zephyrus do), swoop down unpredictably in wild, random gusts, now here, now there. With the Titans routed and Typhon overthrown, Zeus takes sovereignty upon himself, at the urging of the gods, and assumes the throne of the immortals. He then distributes responsibilities and honors (*timai*) among the Olympians. In the same way Marduk, on being proclaimed king of the gods, killed Tiamat and cut his corpse in two, flinging half of it into the air to form the sky; then he established the positions and movements of the stars, fixed the year and the months, ordained time and space, created the human race, and distributed privileges and destinies.

These resemblances between Greek theogony and the Babylonian creation myth are not accidental. Cornford's hypothesis of a borrowing has been confirmed—but also modified and rounded out—by the recent discovery of two series of documents: the Phoenician tablets of Ras Shamra, from the beginning of the fourteenth century B.C., and some fifteenth-century Hittite texts in cuneiform which recapitulate an ancient Hurrian saga. The almost simultaneous discovery of these two sets of documents has revealed a whole series of new convergences that explain the presence of details that had seemed out of place or incomprehensible in the web of the Hesiodic account. The problem of eastern influences on Greek origin myths—their scope and limits, how and when they first appeared—is here posed in precise and concrete fashion.

In these eastern theogonies, as in the Greek theogonies that were modeled on them, the genesis themes remain integrated with a vast royal epic that depicts the clash of successive generations of gods and various sacred powers for dominion over the world. The institution of sovereign power and the establishment of order appear as two inseparable aspects of the same divine drama, the stakes in a single struggle, the fruit of a single victory. This general feature marks the subordination of the mythic tale to the royal rituals of which it had been an element from the beginning, and of which it was the oral accompaniment. Thus the Babylonian poem of the Creation, the *Enuma elish*, was sung every year in Babylon on the fourth day of the royal festival of the Creation of the New Year, in the month of Nisan. On that date, time was supposed to have completed its cycle and the world returned to its starting point—a critical moment at which the whole order was again threatened. During the festival the king mimed a ritual combat against a dragon. Thus each year he repeated the feat performed by Marduk against Tiamat at the beginning of the world. The ordeal and the royal victory had a double significance: even as they confirmed the power of the monarch's sovereignty, they symbolized a re-creation of the cosmic, seasonal, and social order. Thanks to the

111

king's religious attributes, the structure of the universe, after a period of crisis, was renewed and upheld for a new temporal cycle.

Babylonian ritual and myth reveal a particular conception of the relation between sovereignty and order. The king not only governed the social hierarchy, but also intervened in the workings of natural phenomena. The ordering of space, the creation of time, and the regulation of the seasonal cycle appear to have been part of the royal activity; these were aspects of the sovereign's function. No distinction was made between nature and society; in all its forms and all its spheres, order was made dependent on the monarch. In neither the human group nor the universe was it yet thought of abstractly or as existing in and of itself. To exist, it would have had to be established; to endure, it would have to be maintained; always it presupposed an ordering agent, a creative power capable of promoting it. Within the framework of this mythic thought one could not imagine an autonomous realm of nature or a principle of organization immanent in the universe.

In Greece, Hesiod's *Theogony* was not alone in having a general design that accorded with this perspective; so do more highly elaborated cosmogonies such as that of Pherecydes of Syros, whom Aristotle placed among the theologians who mingled philosophy with myth. If Pherecydes, a contemporary of Anaximander, kept the traditional figures of the major divinities, he nonetheless transformed their names by etymological word play to suggest or emphasize their attributes as natural forces. Kronos becomes Chronos (Time); Rhea, Re, which evokes the notion of flux or flow; Zeus is called Zas, perhaps to indicate the magnitude of sovereign power. But the myth continued to center on the theme of a struggle for the lordship of the universe. So far as we can tell from the fragments that have come down to us, Pherecydes gave an account of the battle of Kronos against Ophion, the clash between their two armies, and the plunge of the vanquished into the ocean, leaving Kronos to reign over the sky. Then came the attack by Zeus, his seizure of power, and his solemn union with Chthonie, with the mediation or assistance of Eros. With the *hieros gamos* [sacred marriage] of Zeus the ruler with the goddess of the underworld, the visible world emerged, and for the first time a model of the marriage rite as *anakalypteria*, or "unveiling," was established. By this marriage the somber Chthonie was transformed. She was enveloped in the veil that Zeus had woven and embroidered for her, revealing the outline of the seas and the contours of the land. Accepting the gift offered her by Zeus as a token of her new prerogative (*geras*), the dark goddess of the underworld became Ge, the visible earth. Zeus then assigned to the various divinities their *moira* or portion of the cosmos. He dispatched to Tartaros, in the custody of the winds and tempests, the forces of disorder and *hybris*.

In the theogonies, then, the problem of origin in its strict sense is, if not wholly implicit, at least present in the background. The myth does not ask how an ordered world could arise out of chaos; it answers the question of who was the sovereign god, who had obtained dominion (*anassein, basileuein*) over the universe. In this sense the myth's function was to establish a distinction and a kind of distance between what is first from a tem-

113

poral standpoint and what is first from the standpoint of power—between the principle that exists chronologically at the beginning of the world and the prince who presides over its present arrangement. The myth takes shape within that distance; it makes it the very subject of its tale, retracing the avatars of sovereignty down the line of the divine generations until the moment when a definitive supremacy brings an end to the dramatic elaboration of the *dynasteia*. It must be emphasized that the term *arche*, which was of such importance in philosophical thought, did not belong to the political vocabulary of myth.[5] It was not simply that myth retained its attachment to expressions that were more specifically "royal," but also that the word *arche*, by referring indiscriminately to the first in a temporal series and to primacy in a social hierarchy, abolished the distance on which myth was based. When Anaximander adopted the term, conferring on it for the first time the philosophical sense of an elementary principle, the innovation not only marked the philosopher's rejection of the "monarchical" vocabulary characteristic of myth, but also expressed his wish to bring together what the theologians inevitably separated—to unify to the fullest extent possible that which came first chronologically, that from which things took form, and that which rules and governs the universe. Indeed, for the natural philosopher the world's order could no longer have been established at a given moment by a single agent: the great law that ruled the universe, immanent in *physis*, had to be already present in some way in the original element

[5]In Hesiod, *arche* is used with an exclusively temporal meaning.

from which, little by little, the world emerged. Aristotle, in his *Metaphysics*, points out that for the early poets and "theologians," it was not *hoi protoi*, the original powers— Nyx, Okeanos, Chaos, Ouranos—that wielded *arche* and *basileia* over the world, but Zeus, a latecomer.[6] Anaximander, in contrast, declares that there was nothing that was *arche* with respect to the *apeiron* (since that had always existed), but that the *apeiron* was *arche* for all the rest—that it encompassed (*periechein*) and governed (*kybernan*) everything.[7]

Let us now attempt a general description of the framework within which the Greek theogonies shaped their image of the world.

1. The universe was a hierarchy of powers. As the structural analogue of human society, it could not be correctly represented by a purely spatial schema or described in terms of position, distance, or movement. Its complex and rigorous order expressed relations between agents; it consisted of relations of force, hierarchies of precedence, authority, title, ties of dominance and submission. Its spatial aspects—its cosmic levels and directions—were concerned less with geometrical properties than with differences in function, value, and rank.

2. This order did not emerge inevitably out of the dynamic play of the elements that made up the universe, but was established in a dramatic fashion through the exploits of an agent.

3. The world was governed by the exceptional power of this agent, who was manifestly unequaled and entitled

[6]Aristotle, *Metaphysics*, 1091a33–1091b7.
[7]*Physics*, 203b7.

to preference, on a higher level than the other gods. The myth projects him to the summit of the cosmic structure as its sovereign, and it is his *monarchia* that preserves the balance among the powers that make up the universe, determining for each its place in the hierarchy and fixing its duties, its prerogatives, and its share of honor.

These three features are interdependent, and give the mythic tale its peculiar logic and coherence. They also show its link, in Greece as in the East, with a conception of sovereignty that gives the king control over the order of the seasons, atmospheric phenomena, and the fertility of the soil, of flocks, and of women. The image of the king as master of weather, rainmaker, bestower of natural abundance—an image that in the Mycenaean age conveyed social realities and corresponded to ritual practices—is still visible in some passages of Homer and Hesiod[8] and in such legends as those of Salmoneus and Aeacus. But in the Greek world it could be no more than a survival. After the collapse of the Mycenaean kingship, when the palace-centered system and the figure of the *wanax* had disappeared, nothing remained of the old royal rituals but vestiges whose meaning had been lost. The memory of the king who periodically recreated the order of the world had been obliterated; the bond that had once existed between mythical deeds attributed to a sovereign and the functioning of natural phenomena was no longer so clearly visible. The breakup of sovereignty and the limitation of royal power thus contributed to the separation of myth from the ritual in which it had originally

[8]Homer, *Odyssey*, XIX, 109; Hesiod, *Works and Days*, 225ff.

been rooted. Released from the religious observance on which it had first been the oral commentary, the tale could become more autonomous and disinterested. In certain respects, it prepared for and prefigured the work of philosophy. Even in some passages of Hesiod, the cosmic order was already dissociated from the royal office, freed of any link with ritual. Thus the problem of how order originated is posed in a more self-contained way. The emergence of the world was no longer described in terms of exploit, but as a process of generation by powers whose names directly evoked physical realities: sky, earth, sea, day, night, and so on. Scholars have noted the "naturalistic" emphasis of the beginning of the *Theogony* (lines 116–133), which sets it off from the rest of the poem. But what is perhaps most significant about this first attempt to describe the origin of the cosmos according to a law of spontaneous generation is precisely that it failed. Despite the attempt at conceptual delineation it represents, Hesiod's thought remained the prisoner of its mythic framework. Ouranos, Gaia, and Pontos were indeed physical realities, having the concrete aspects of sky, earth, and sea; but at the same time they were divinities who coupled, reproduced, and behaved generally like human beings. Operating on two levels, thought apprehended the same phenomenon—for example, the separation of the earth from the waters—as simultaneously a natural event in the visible world and a divine childbirth in a primordial time. To break with the vocabulary and logic of myth, Hesiod would have needed a comprehensive idea capable of replacing the mythic schema of a hierarchy of powers ruled by a sovereign.

117

What he did not have was the ability to portray a universe obedient to the rule of law, a cosmos set in order through the application to all its parts of a single order of *isonomia*, consisting of equilibrium, reciprocity, and symmetry.

CHAPTER EIGHT

The New Image
of the World

In assessing the magnitude of the intellectual revolution wrought by the Milesians, we must rely primarily on the work of Anaximander. The doxography[1] gives us a more complete view of it, or at least a less sketchy one, than of the speculations of Thales and Anaximenes. And most important, Anaximander not only added to his vocabulary such an important term as *arche*, but also, by choosing to write in prose, completed the rupture with the poetic style of the theogonies and ushered in a new literary genre suited to *historia peri physeos* [inquiry on nature]. And it is in Anaximander, finally, that we find the most rigorous expression of the new cosmological projection that was to leave a deep and permanent mark on the Greek conception of the universe.

This schema remained genetic. Like *physis* and *genesis*, *arche* kept its temporal meaning of origin or source. The natural philosophers inquired whence and

---

[1]The totality of texts, from the fourth century B.C. to the Christian Era, reporting the opinions of the ancient philosophers. [Editor's note.]

by what path the world had come into being. But this genetic reconstruction accounted for the formation of an order that was now projected within a spatial framework. Here one point must be emphasized. The Milesians' debt to Babylonian astronomy is undeniable. From it they took not only the observations and methods that permitted Thales to predict an eclipse, according to legend, but also such instruments as the *gnomon*, which Anaximander is said to have brought to Sparta. The resumption of contacts with the East proved, once more, to be decisive in the unleashing of a Greek science in which astronomical concerns played a major role from the outset. And yet Greek astronomy, with its geometrical (no longer arithmetical) cast and its secular character free of all astral religion, was from the start on a different plane from that of the Babylonian science that inspired it. The Ionians located the order of the cosmos in space; they imagined the structure of the universe and the positions, distances, dimensions, and movements of the stars according to geometric patterns. Just as they sketched on a *pinax* [wooden tablet] a map of the whole earth, putting on public view the shape of the inhabited world, with its lands, its seas, and its rivers, so they constructed mechanical models of the universe, such as the sphere that Anaximander is said to have made. In thus presenting the cosmos "for inspection," they made of it, in the fullest sense of the term, a *theoria*, a spectacle.

This conception of the physical universe in geometric terms entailed a general reordering of cosmological perspectives; it sanctioned the advent of a form of thought and an explanatory system that had no analogy in myth. To take one example, Anaximander placed a motionless earth at the center of the universe. He explained that if the earth stayed at rest in that place, with no need for support, it was because it was equidistant from all points on the celestial circumference, and so had no more reason to sink than to rise, or to move to one side rather than the other. Anaximander thus located the cosmos in a mathematical space composed of purely geometrical relationships. With one stroke he obliterated the mythic image of a layered world, where the absolute opposition of high and low marked the cosmic levels that differentiated the divine powers, and whose spatial directions had contrasting religious meanings. Furthermore, all the explanations by which myth sought to affirm the stability of the earth, a "firm foundation for all the living" (Hesiod), were revealed as useless and ridiculous: the earth no longer needed "support" or "roots"; it no longer had to float (as for Thales) on the liquid element from which it allegedly arose, or to rest on a whirlpool or (as for Anaximenes) a cushion of air. Everything was clear, everything had been said, once the spatial schema had been defined. To understand why human beings could walk on the ground in complete safety and why the earth did not fall as objects on its surface do, it was enough to know that all the radii of a circle are equal.

Its geometrical structure gave the cosmos a kind of organization that was contrary to the one ascribed to it by myth. No longer was any element or portion of the world to be privileged at the expense of the rest; no longer was any physical power to be in the dominant position of a *basileus* exercising his *dynasteia* over all things. Since the earth was located at the center of a perfectly circular universe, it could remain motionless by reason of its equidistance, without submitting to the domination of anything whatever: *hypo medenos kratoumene*. This formula of Anaximander's, which includes the idea of *kratos*, the power of domination over others, shows the persistence of political concepts and vocabulary in the Ionians' cosmological thought. But as Charles H. Kahn very rightly emphasizes in a recent study, Anaximander here upheld a thesis that went well beyond the one later advanced by his disciple Anaximenes.[2] For Anaximenes, the earth had to rest on the air, which dominated it *(synkratei)* as the soul dominated the body. For Anaximander, in contrast, no single element, no portion of the world could dominate the others. It was the equality and symmetry of the various powers that made up the cosmos that characterized the new natural order. Supremacy belonged exclusively to a law of equilibrium and continuous reciprocity. *Monarchia* was replaced, in nature as in the city, by a rule of *isonomia*.

From this concept came the refusal to confer the power of *arche* on water (with Thales), on air (with Anaximenes), or on any other particular element. Anaximander conceived the first substance—"infinite, immortal, and divine, covering and governing" everything—as a reality apart, distinct from all the elements; it formed their common origin and was the inexhaustible source from which all fed equally. Aristotle gives us the reasons for this choice: if one of the elements had the infinity that belonged to the *apeiron*, the others

---

[2]Charles H. Kahn, *Anaximander and the Origins of Greek Cosmology* (New York, 1960).

would be destroyed by it. The elements, indeed, were defined by their reciprocal opposition, and so they must always be in a relationship of equality (*isazei aei tanantia*) with one another, or as Aristotle would say elsewhere, in an equality of powers (*isotes tes dynameos*).[3] There is no reason to doubt the relevance of Aristotle's reasoning or to reject his interpretation of Anaximander's thought. We may note that Aristotle's argument implies a radical change in the relations between power and order. *Basileia* and *monarchia*, which had established and maintained order in myth, appeared destructive of order in Anaximander's new perspective. Order was no longer hierarchical, but lay in the maintenance of equilibrium between powers that were now equal, no one of which must dominate the others so completely that the cosmos would be destroyed. If the *apeiron* held *arche* and governed all things, it was precisely because its reign excluded the possibility that any one element could seize *dynasteia*. The primacy of the *apeiron* guaranteed the permanence of an egalitarian order based on the reciprocity of relations, an order that was superior to all the elements and governed them equally.

Moreover, this equilibrium of forces was by no means static; it encompassed opposition, it was formed out of conflict. Each force prevailed in turn, seizing power and then falling back, yielding it up in proportion to its earlier advance. In the universe, in the progression of seasons, in the human body, supremacy thus passed from one to the other in a regular cycle, linking together dominance and submission, expansion and contraction, strength

[3]Aristotle, *Physics*, 204b22 and 13-19; *Meteorologica*, 340a16.

and weakness, birth and death, like symmetrical and reversible poles. For Anaximander all elements "mutually and in sequence offer to one another reparation *(tisis)* and justice *(dike)* for the *adikia* [injustice] they have committed."

A world made up of opposed and endlessly conflicting *dynameis* subjected them to a rule of compensatory justice, an order that preserved them in exact *isotes* [equality]. Under the yoke of a *dike* that is the same for all, the elementary forces are connected and coordinated in a regular rhythm, so that despite their multiplicity and diversity, they form a single cosmos.

Anaximander delineated this new image of the world so rigorously that it formed a sort of common ground for the pre-Socratic philosophers as a whole and for medical thought as well. At the beginning of the fifth century, Alcmeon formulated it in terms that expressed its political origin so clearly that it seems unnecessary to dwell on it further, especially after the articles that A. G. Vlastos has devoted to the question.[4] Alcmeon, indeed, defined health as *isonomia ton dynameon*, a balance of powers—wet and dry, cold and hot, bitter and sweet, and so on; sickness resulted from the *monarchia* of one element over the rest, since the exclusive rule of one particular element was destructive.

But social experience did not simply provide cos-

---

[4] A. G. Vlastos, "Equality and Justice in Early Greek Cosmologies," *Classical Philology*, 42 (1947), 156–178; "Theology and Philosophy in Early Greek Thought," *Philosophical Quarterly*, 1952, pp. 97–123; "Isonomia," *American Journal of Philology*, 74 (1953), 337–366; and the review of the work of F. M. Cornford, *Principium Sapientiae*, in *Gnomon*, 27 (1955), 65–76.

mological thought with the model of an egalitarian law and order in place of the all-powerful rule of the monarch. As we have seen, the government of the city was bound up with a new conception of space: the institutions of the *polis* were designed and embodied in what may be called a political space. We may note that the first urban planners, such as Hippodamus of Miletus, were in fact political theorists: the organization of urban space was but one aspect of a more general effort to order and rationalize the human world. The link between the city's space and its institutions still appears very clearly in the works of Plato and Aristotle.

The new social space was organized around a center. *Kratos, arche,* and *dynasteia* were no longer to be found at the top of the social scale; they were located *es meson,* at the center, in the middle of the human group. It was this center that now was valued; the welfare of the *polis* rested on those who were known as *hoi mesoi,* because, being equidistant from the extremes, they constituted a fixed point on which the city was balanced. Individuals and groups all occupied symmetrical positions in relation to this center. The agora, which represented this spatial arrangement on the ground, formed the center of a common public space. All those who entered it were by that fact defined as equals, *isoi.* By their presence in that political space they entered into relations of perfect reciprocity with one another. The institution of the *hestia koine,* the public hearth, was a symbol of this political community.[5] Established in the prytaneum, which was usually on the

[5]See L. Gernet, "Sur le symbolisme politique en Grèce ancienne: Le foyer commun," *Cahiers internationaux de Sociologie,* 11 (1951), 21–43.

agora, this public hearth, with its link to the many domestic hearths, became in a sense equidistant from the various families that made up the city; it represented them all without being identified with any one in particular. The social space was a centered space—common, public, egalitarian, and symmetrical—but also secularized, intended for confrontation, debate, and argument; it contrasted with the Acropolis, a religiously designated space, as the province of the *hosia*, the city's profane concerns, contrasted with that of the *hiera*, the sacred matters that concerned the gods.

That this new spatial framework facilitated the geometrical orientation of Greek astronomy—that there was a profound structural analogy between the institutional space in which the human cosmos was expressed and the physical space in which the Milesians projected the natural cosmos—is suggested by a comparison of certain texts.

According to the doxography, if the earth could remain fixed and motionless for Anaximander, it was because of its central position *(peri meson, mese)*, its correspondence *(homoiotes)*, and its balance *(isorropia)*. Since it was in the center, Anaximander said, it was not ruled *(kratoumene)* by anything. What Anaximander saw as the link, for us so paradoxical, of the absence of "rule" with centrality and correspondence permits a comparison with a political text by Herodotus, in which we find the same vocabulary and the same conceptual interdependence. Herodotus writes that at the death of the tyrant Polycrates, Maeandrius—named by the dead man to bear the *skeptron* after him—called all the citizens together and announced his decision to abolish the tyranny: "I never approved," he told them in substance, "of Polycrates' reigning as a despot over men who were his equals [*despozon andron homoion heauto*]. . . . For myself, I lay down the *arche es meson*, at the center, and I proclaim *isonomia* for you."[6]

The comparison appears all the more meaningful since for the Milesians themselves the conception of physical space symmetrically organized about a center corresponds to certain images of the social order. According to Agathemerus, Anaximander of Miletus, disciple of Thales, was the first to draw the inhabited earth on a *pinax*, as Hecataeus of Miletus was to do more precisely after him.[7] The author adds that the ancients represented the inhabited earth as round, with Greece at the center, and Delphi at the center of Greece. We know that this notion roused Herodotus to irony: "I laugh," he wrote, "when I see the maps of the world that many people have drawn in the past, and which no one has sensibly explained. They drew the ocean running around the earth, which was round as though it had been done with a compass, and they made Asia as big as Europe."[8] In another passage Herodotus reveals the institutional and political background of this geometrization of physical space, which in his opinion had been carried too far: after disaster had befallen the Ionians, they all gathered at the Panionion. First Bias of Priene, one of the sages, advised that they form a joint fleet to sail to Sardinia and found there a single Panionian city. Thales of Miletus was the next to speak. He proposed that they have a single

[6]Herodotus, III, 142.
[7]Agathemerus, I, 1.
[8]Herodotus, IV, 36.

council (*hen Bouleuterion*) and locate its seat at Teos, since that island was at the center of Ionia *(meson Ionies)*; the other cities would continue to be inhabited, but would henceforth be in the position of outlying demes incorporated into a single *polis*. [9]

We have still further evidence of the confusion that could be produced among the political, geometrical, and physical meanings of the center when that center was conceived of as the fixed point around which an egalitarian space, made up of symmetrical and reversible relations, was arranged in both society and nature. [10] Hestia, the symbol of the new human order on the agora, could signify for Philolaos the central cosmic fire, for other philosophers the earth that sits motionless in the middle of the physical universe. [11]

In the fourth century Plato was still very much aware of these correspondences between the structure of the natural cosmos and the organization of the social cosmos. The philosopher who had inscribed at the entrance to the Academy, "Let no one enter here who is not a geometer," bears witness to the links between geometrical thought

---

[9]Herodotus, I, 170.

[10]Of course, mythological thought was familiar with the ideas of circularity and center; it, too, attributed value to both. But the religious image of the center did not entail a symmetrical space; rather, it implied a hierarchical space made up of cosmic levels that could communicate with each other through the center. The political symbolism of the center (the common hearth) appeared as a kind of mediation between the religious idea of the center *(omphalos, hestia)* and the geometrical concept of the center in a homogeneous space. On this point see L. Gernet, "Sur le symbolisme politique," pp. 42ff.

[11]See R. E. Siegel, "On the Relation between Early Scientific Thought and Mysticism: Is Hestia, the Central Fire, an Abstract Astronomical Concept?," *Janus*, 49 (1960), 1-20.

and political thought which a common origin and orientation had established and long maintained among the Greeks. Excoriating in the *Gorgias* all those who refused to study geometry (in the person of Callicles and from the mouth of Socrates), Plato closely allied the knowledge of *isotes*—geometrical equality, the foundation of the physical cosmos—with *dikaiosyne* and *sophrosyne*, the political virtues on which the new order of the city was based:

> And wise men tell us, Callicles, that heaven and earth and gods and men are held together by communion [*koinonia*] and friendship [*philia*], by orderliness [*cosmiotes*], temperance [*sophrosyne*], and justice [*dikaiotes*]. . . . Now you, as it seems to me, do not give proper attention to this, for all your cleverness, but have failed to observe the great power of geometrical equality amongst both gods and men: you hold that self-advantage is what one ought to practice, because you neglect geometry.[12]

[12]Plato, *Gorgias*, 508a [English translation by W. R. M. Lamb (Cambridge, Mass., and London: Loeb Classical Library, 1939)].

Conclusion

The advent of the *polis*, the birth of philosophy—the two sequences of phenomena are so closely linked that the origin of rational thought must be seen as bound up with the social and mental structures peculiar to the Greek city. Thus restored to its historical setting, philosophy casts off the character of pure revelation that scholars have sometimes bestowed upon it, proclaiming that in the youthful science of the Ionians timeless Reason became incarnate in Time. The Milesian school did not witness the birth of Reason; rather, it devised a kind of reasoning, an early form of rationality. This Greek reason is not the experimental rationalism of contemporary science, oriented toward exploration of the physical environment and making use of the methods, intellectual tools, and mental structures that have been worked out during the past few centuries in the laborious effort to understand and control nature. When Aristotle defined man as a "political animal," he emphasized what differentiates Greek reason from today's reason. If in his eyes *Homo sapiens* was *Homo politicus*, it was because Reason itself was in essence political.

130

In fact, it was at the political level that Reason was first expressed, established, and shaped in Greece. Social experience could become the object of pragmatic thought for the Greeks because in the city-state it lent itself to public debate. The decline of myth dates from the day the first sages brought human order under discussion and sought to define it, to render it in formulas accessible to the intelligence, and to apply to it the standard of measure and number. Thus evolved a strictly political thought, separate from religion, with its own vocabulary, concepts, principles, and theoretical aims. That thought profoundly affected the mentality of ancient human beings; it characterized a civilization that to the very end never ceased to consider public life the pinnacle of human activity. For the Greeks, the individual could not be separated from the citizen; *phronesis*, reflection, was the privilege of free men, who exercised their reason and their civic rights at one and the same time. By thus providing citizens with the framework within which they conceived their reciprocal relations, political thought at once directed and shaped their thinking in other areas.

When philosophy arose at Miletus, it was rooted in the political thought whose fundamental preoccupations it expressed and from which it borrowed a part of its vocabulary. It is true that quite soon it claimed greater independence. With Parmenides it took its own path; it explored a new domain and posed problems unique to itself. The philosophers no longer inquired, as the Milesians had done, into the nature of order and how it was created and maintained, but into the nature of Being and Knowing and the relations between them. The Greeks thus added a new dimension to the history of human thought. To clear up the theoretical difficulties, the *aporiai* brought about by its very development, philosophy had little by little to invent a language, elaborate its concepts, erect a logic, construct its own rationality. But in this task it kept its distance from physical reality; it drew little on observation of natural phenomena; it conducted no experiments. The very idea of experimentation remained foreign to it. It developed a mathematics but made no attempt to use it to explore nature. It failed to make the connection between mathematics and natural philosophy, between calculation and experiment—a connection that seems to us to have linked geometry and politics from the start. For Greek thought, if the social world could be subject to number and measure, nature represented rather the realm of the approximate, to which neither exact calculation nor rigorous reasoning could be applied. Greek reason was not so much the product of human commerce with things as of the relations of human beings with one another. It developed less through the techniques that apply to the world than through those that give one person a hold over others, and whose common instrument is language: the art of the politician, the rhetorician, the pedagogue. Greek reason is that reason which makes it possible to act practically, deliberately, and systematically on human beings, not to transform nature. In its limitations as in its innovations, it is a creature of the city.

Readings

1. The Historical Background

V. Gordon Childe, *The Dawn of European Civilization*, 6th ed. (London, 1957); H. L. Lorimer, *Homer and the Monuments* (London, 1950); A. Severyns, *Grèce et Proche-Orient avant Homère* (Brussels, 1960); Sterling Dow, "The Greeks in the Bronze Age," in *Rapports du XIe Congrès international des sciences historiques*, 2, *Antiquité* (Uppsala, 1960), pp. 1-34; Denys L. Page, *History and Homeric Iliad* (Berkeley and Los Angeles, 1959); *The Aegean and the Near East: Studies Presented to Hetty Goldman* (New York, 1956).

2. Mycenaean Royalty

John Chadwick, *The Decipherment of Linear B* (Cambridge, Eng., 1958); *Etudes mycéniennes: Actes du Colloque international sur les textes mycéniens* (Paris, 1956); L. R. Palmer, *Achaeans and Indo-Europeans* (Oxford, 1955); M. Ventris and J. Chadwick, *Documents in Mycenaean Greek* (Cambridge, Eng., 1956).

On social structures and the system of land tenure: W. E. Brown, "Land-Tenure in Mycenaean Pylos," *Historia*, 5 (1956), 385-400; E. L. Bennett, "The Landholders of Pylos," *American Journal of Archaeology*, 60 (1956), 103-133; M. I. Finley, "Homer and Mycenae: Property and Tenure," *Historia*, 6 (1957), 133-

159, and "The Mycenaean Tablets and Economic History," *Economic History Review*, 2d ser., 10 (1957), 128–141 (with a reply by L. R. Palmer, *Economic History Review*, 2d ser., 11 [1958], 87–96); M. S Ruiperez, "Mycenaean Land-Division and Livestock Grazing," *Minos*, 5, 174–207; G. Thomson, "On Greek Land Tenure," in *Studies Robinson*, II, 840–857; E. Will, "Aux origines du régime foncier grec," *Revue des Etudes anciennes*, 59 (1957), 5–50.

7. Cosmogonies and Myths of Sovereignty

On the origins of Greek thought and the beginnings of philosophic reflection, see John Burnet, *Early Greek Philosophy*, 3d ed. (London, 1920); F. M. Cornford, *From Religion to Philosophy: A Study in the Origins of Western Speculation* (London, 1912) and *Principium Sapientiae: The Origins of Greek Philosophical Thought* (Cambridge, Eng., 1952); H. Fränkel, *Dichtung und Philosophie des frühens Griechentums* (New York, 1951) and *Wege und Formen frühgriechischen Denkens* (Munich, 1955); L. Gernet, "Les origines de la philosophie," *Bulletin de l'Enseignement public du Maroc*, 183 (1945), 9ff.; O. Gigon, *Der Ursprung der griechischen Philosophie von Hesiod bis Parmenides* (Basel, 1945); W. K. C. Guthrie, *In the Beginning: Some Greek Views on the Origins of Life and the Early State of Man* (London, 1957); W. Jaeger, *The Theology of the Early Greek Philosophers* (Oxford, 1947); G. S. Kirk and J. E. Raven, *The Presocratic Philosophers: A Critical History with a Selection of Texts* (Cambridge, Eng., 1957); W. Nestle, *Vom Mythos zum Logos: Die Selbstentfaltung des griechischen Denkens von Homer bis auf die Sophistik und Sokrates* (Stuttgart, 1940); R. B. Onians, *The Origins of European Thought about the Body, the Mind, the Soul, the World, Time, and Fate* (Cambridge, Eng., 1951); P.-M. Schuhl, *Essai sur la formation de la pensée grecque: Introduction historique à une étude de la philosophie platonicienne* (Paris, 1934; 2d ed. 1948); B. Snell, *Die Entdeckung des Geistes: Studien zur Entstehung des europäischen Denkens bei den Griechen*, 2d ed. (Hamburg, 1948) [published in English as *The Discovery of the Mind: The Greek Origins of European Thought*, trans. T. G. Rosenmeyer (Cambridge, Mass.: Harvard University Press, 1950; New York: Harper Torchbooks, 1960)]; G. Thomson, *The First Philosophers*, vol. 2 of *Studies in Ancient Greek Society* (London, 1955), and "From Religion to Philosophy," *Journal of Hellenic Studies*, 73 (1953), 77-84; J.-P. Vernant, "Du mythe à la raison: La formation de la pensée positive dans la Grèce archaïque," *Annales: Economies, Sociétés, Civilisations*, 1957, pp. 183-206.

On the relations between Greek and Near Eastern theogonies, see R. D. Barnett, "The Epic of Kumarbi and the *Theogony* of Hesiod," *Journal of Hellenic Studies*, 65 (1945), 100-101; J. Duchemin, "Sources grecques et orientales de la *Théogonie* d'Hésiode," *L'Information littéraire*, 1952, pp. 146-151; R. Dussaud, "Antécédents orientaux à la *Théogonie* d'Hésiode," *Mélanges Grégoire*, 1 (1949), 226-231; O. Eissfeldt, "Phönikische und griechische Kosmogonie," in *Eléments orientaux dans la religion grecque ancienne* (Paris, 1960), pp. 1-55; E. O. Forrer, "Eine Geschichte des Götterkönigtums aus dem Hatti-Reiche," *Mélanges Fr. Cumont*, 1936, pp. 687-713; H. G Güterbock, "The Hittite Version of the Hurrian Kumarpi Myths: Oriental Forerunners of Hesiod," *American Journal of Archaeology*, 52 (1948), 123-134; H. Schwabe, "Die griechischen Theogonien und der Orient," in *Eléments orientaux dans la religion grecque ancienne*, pp. 39-56; F. Vian, "Le mythe de Typhée et le problème de ses origines orientales," in *Eléments orientaux dans la religion grecque ancienne*, pp. 17-37, and "Influences orientales et survivances indo-européennes dans la *Théogonie* d'Hésiode," *Revue de la Franco-ancienne*, 126 (1958), 329-336; S. Wikander, "Histoire des Ouranides," *Cahiers du Sud*, 314 (1952), 9-17. Also available are Near Eastern texts edited by J. B Pritchard, *Ancient Near Eastern Texts Relating to the Old Testament*, 2d ed. (Princeton, 1955).

Index

Index

Index

141

Index

Index